WOMAN OF VALOR

A RESTORATIVE JOURNEY

DEBORAH IRELAND DOUGLAS

RESTORE-U PUBLICATIONS
WEST DES MOINES, IOWA

Copyright©2013 Deborah Ireland Douglas

2013 by Restore-U Publications

Illustrations and Cover: Jolene Crafton
Copyright©2013 Jolene Crafton

Printed: United States of America

All rights reserved. No part of this publication may be reproduced, stored in a retrieval system, or transmitted in any form or by any means – for example, electronic, photocopy, recording – without prior written permission from the publisher. The only exception is brief quotations in printed reviews.

Unless otherwise noted, all Scripture quotations are from the New Living Translation copyright 1996 by Restore-U Publications. Used by permission from Tyndale House Publishers, Inc. All rights reserved.

Scripture quotations identified as RSV are from the Revised Standard Version of the Bible, copyright 1974 by Plume. Used by permission.

Albert Einstein, *The Ultimate Quotable Einstein*. Princeton: Princeton University Press, 2010.

To my sisters, S.A.L.T.
(Sisters All Learning Together)

Who Learn, Laugh, Encourage,
Pray, and Cry
together weekly at
Lutheran Church of Hope

And to Jolene who tries really hard to keep my
feet on the ground
(and who did incredible illustrations).

CONTENTS

Introduction   Proverbs 31:10

Unit 1-Exploring who God made ME to Be
The Woman at the Well/Proverbs 31:11-12, 30
- Chapter 1 - Relational — 7
- Chapter 2 - Spiritual — 14
- Chapter 3 – Relational and Spiritual — 19

Unit II Exploring YOUR Personal Space
Mary the Mother of Jesus/Proverbs 31:25-26 — 25
- Chapter 4 – Character — 27
- Chapter 5 – Gifts — 32
- Chapter 6 - YOU — 40
- Chapter 7 – Adversity — 45

Unit III   Exploring YOUR Living Space
Mary and Martha and Proverbs 31:13-19 — 51
- Chapter 8 - YOUR space — 53
- Chapter 9 - Easy Changes — 58

Unit IV – Exploring Communication
The Woman Bleeding and Proverbs 31:27-29 — 65
- Chapter 10 – Women — 67
- Chapter 11 – Men — 72

Unit V - Creative Exploration
Mary Magdalene and Proverbs 31:21-24 — 78
- Chapter 12 -Creative Capacities — 80
- Chapter 13 - YOUR Genius — 85

Unit VI – Exploring Learning
Adulterous Woman and Proverbs 31:20 — 90
- Chapter 14 - How We Think — 92
- Chapter 15 - Changing Attitudes — 99

Unit VII - Love and Faith
Anna and Proverbs 31:10 — 105
- Chapter 16 – Loving — 107
- Chapter 17 – Faithfulness — 115

Postlude - Thankfulness — 124

INTRODUCTION

Who are you? Inside and out...

Are you a woman after God's heart? Do you thirst to receive more of God? Thirst restoration from the destruction of this world? Do you yearn to sit in the arms of God and experience His peace that passes all understanding?

If you are, you're in the right place...

We will explore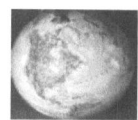

Godly Character

        Inner Beauty

    Creativity

    Relational Communication

    Compassion

Being a woman after God's heart doesn't mean you possess all of those characteristics. It means you passionately love God and you long for a fuller life IN God.

Consider unpacking what that looks like for YOU – write a love letter to God, pouring out your heart with all of your hopes and desires – and place the letter on this page for future reference.

Exploring God

What are the characteristics of God?

Triune: Father, Son, Spirit

All powerful, All loving, Eternal (Alpha and Omega), Gives Complete Forgiveness FREE, All knowing, Constantly Pursues US with love, Perfect Communicator, Comforter, Creator, Sustainer, Counselor, Everything...

Hebrew Woman

King Lemeul's mother outlines in Proverbs 31:10-31 an ideal Hebrew woman. She tells her son that this woman can multi-task by spinning wool, sewing garments, and selling those garments. She is relational and she can be trusted by her husband. She cares for her family from morning to night and she remembers the poor and broken. The King's mother advises her son to seek out a woman who seeks God's face. She is good and kind to all. She is not a chatty woman…she listens well and speaks wisdom.

She carries herself with inner beauty, is dignified, caring, communicates relationally, and is compassionate.

Because she is a Godly woman, she is unafraid of what tomorrow holds for her and her family. (There is a quote, "Don't worry about tomorrow because God's already been there.") She knew God had everything covered (Psalm 23:1 in the NLT).

Proverb 31 is poetry, and the characteristics of the woman serve as an example of God's loving wisdom through the Spirit. God desires that women will receive His wisdom.

Exploring the world's ideal 21st Century Woman:
Tall, blonde, thin yet curvy, witty, and sensual. She is expected to do it all, look her best all the time, and like everyone. Women tend to be more concerned about pleasing others, being polite, and are expected to be nice. She is not supposed to get angry in public, stand up for herself, tell the whole truth, or say "no" when someone says they need her.

Is that picture the same as the model God gives in Proverb 31?
How does the Proverbs 31 model differ?

Exploring You IN God

Characteristics of Women:
Uniquely wired

Scientists have found that as a fetus forms the brain the male of the species forms "blocks" that separate areas. That allows men to compartmentalize. A female brain doesn't form these blocks and her brain develops a continuous flow of thought that touches other areas of the brain. As a result, a woman can naturally relate everything in her thought patterns. There are definite advantages to both; but we are uniquely created for God's good purpose IN us.

So, what is the truth about what God desires from a woman?

God desires that she is given and receives love, affection, and encouragement. In order to receive God's love women need to spend time with God. It's best if we do not always have an "agenda".

With a woman's unique brain, generally speaking, God gave us special abilities* with:

Doing more than one thing at a time

Relationships

Communicating well   Nurturing

    Offering Compassion

[5]

*While there are men who have some of those characteristics and women who do only some of those well, women have the capacity to communicate their emotions to the family.

God wants women to embrace their inner beauty and the calling they have on their lives. Our outer beauty springs from within and while there is nothing wrong with wanting to look nice on the outside, God's first concern is for our relationship with Him. True inner beauty comes from a Godly connection, a Godly heart, God's joy, peace, patience, goodness, kindness, and self-control (Galatians 5:22). God also desires that women receive His wisdom. James 1:5 promises those who ask for wisdom will receive wisdom.

God intended for women to be treated with care and affection and did not intend for women to be abused or treated carelessly. It is never God's intention for anyone to be abused. God's intention for women and men is that they would be restored in His love.*

Emmanuel – God with us – Jesus treated women with honor and respect. As we proceed with our look at what God intended for women we are going to look at the women in Jesus' life through the lens of the Proverbs 31 woman.

*That's what Restore-U.org is all about.

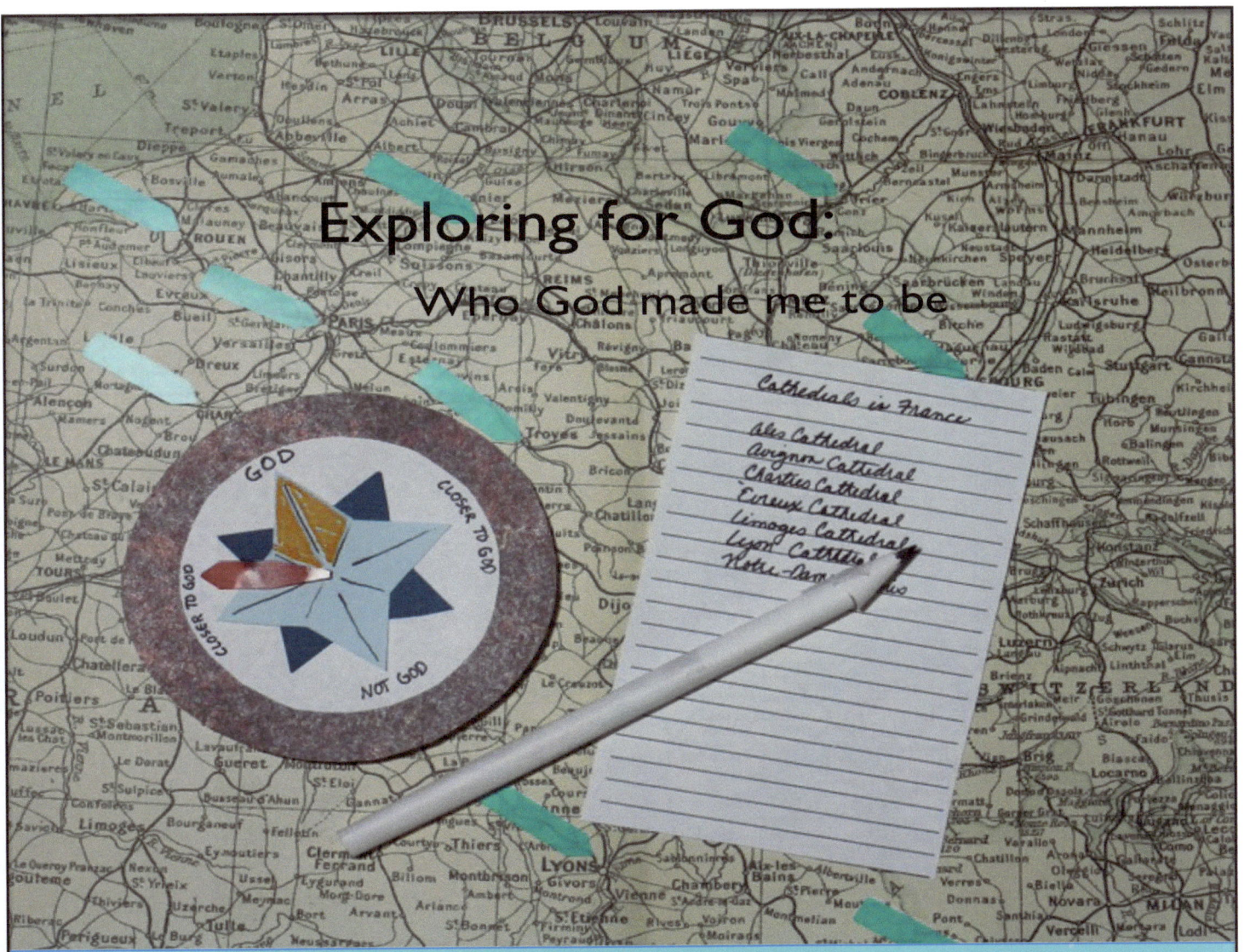

UNIT 1

CHAPTERS 1-3

RELATIONAL
SPIRITUAL

Proverbs 31:10-31:
10 Who can find a virtuous and capable wife? She is more precious than rubies.
11 Her husband can trust her, and she will greatly enrich his life.
12 She brings him good, not harm, all the days of her life.
13 She finds wool and flax and busily spins it.
14 She is like a merchant's ship, bringing her food from afar.
15 She gets up before dawn to prepare breakfast for her household and plan the day's work for her servant girls.
16 She goes to inspect a field and buys it; with her earnings she plants a vineyard.
17 She is energetic and strong, a hard worker.
18 She makes sure her dealings are profitable; her lamp burns late into the night.
19 Her hands are busy spinning thread, her fingers twisting fiber.
20 She extends a helping hand to the poor and opens her arms to the needy.
21 She has no fear of winter for her household, for everyone has warm clothes.
22 She makes her own bedspreads. She dresses in fine linen and purple gowns.
23 Her husband is well known at the city gates, where he sits with the other civic leaders.
24 She makes belted linen garments and sashes to sell to the merchants.
25 She is clothed with strength and dignity, and she laughs without fear of the future.
26 When she speaks, her words are wise, and she gives instructions with kindness.
27 She carefully watches everything in her household and suffers nothing from laziness.
28 Her children stand and bless her. Her husband praises her:
29 "There are many virtuous and capable women in the world, but you surpass them all!"
30 Charm is deceptive, and beauty does not last; but a woman who fears the Lord will be greatly praised.
31 Reward her for all she has done. Let her deeds publicly declare her praise. (NLT)

UNIT 1

EXPLORING WHO GOD MADE ME TO BE

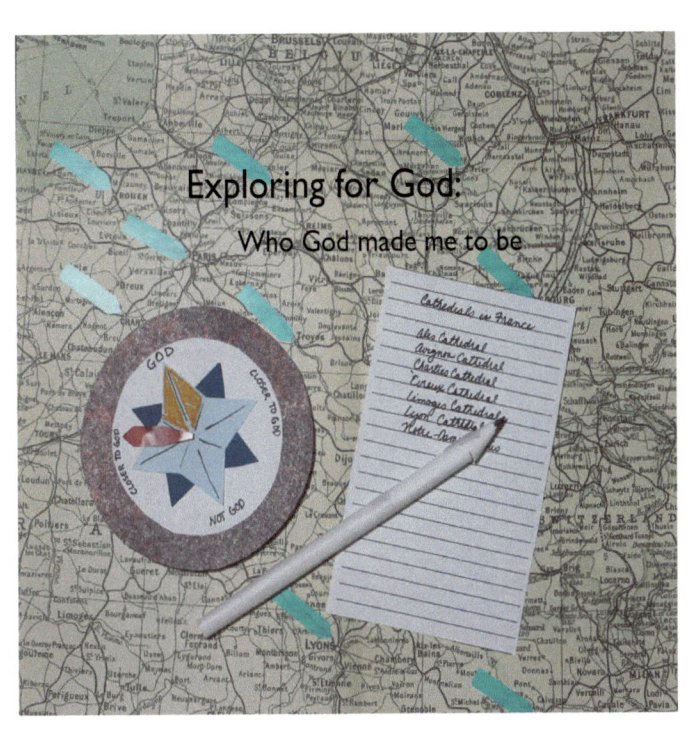

CHAPTER 1
RELATIONAL

WOMAN OF VALOR
THE WOMAN AT THE WELL

Exploring for God:
Who God made me to be

John 4:3-15

He (Jesus) left Judea and departed again to Galilee. He had to pass through Samar'ia. So he came to a city of Samar'ia, called Sy'char, near the field that Jacob gave to his son Joseph. Jacob's well was there, and so Jesus, wearied as he was with his journey, sat down beside the well. It was about the sixth hour.

There came a woman of Samar'ia to draw water. Jesus said to her, "Give me a drink." For his disciples had gone away into the city to buy food.

The Samaritan woman said to him, "How is it that you, a Jew, ask a drink of me, a woman of Samar'ia?" For Jews have no dealings with Samaritans. Jesus answered her, "If you knew the gift of God, and who it is that is saying to you, 'Give me a drink,' you would have asked him, and he would have given you living water."

The woman said to him, "Sir, you have nothing to draw with, and the well is deep; where do you get that living water? Are you greater than our father Jacob, who gave us the well, and drank from it himself, and his sons, and his cattle?"

Jesus said to her, "Every one who drinks of this water will thirst again, but whoever drinks of the water that I shall give him will never thirst; the water that I shall give him will become in him a spring of water welling up to eternal life." The woman said to him, "Sir, give me this water, that I may not thirst, nor come here to draw." (RSV)

The Samaritan woman who came to the well at the sixth hour of the day (around noon instead of early morning) probably did so because she was avoiding the other women in town. Since the other women in town would have known about her past, she was avoiding their comments and judgments about her life choices.

Has there been a time in your life when you felt like you were being judged, or you knew others were gossiping about you? How did that made you feel?

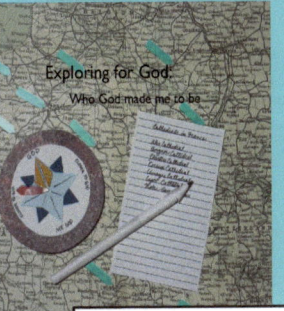

By making the choice to speak with the Samaritan woman, Jesus was stepping outside the boundaries of what was considered acceptable within the Jewish culture.

The Samaritan woman only saw their differences and she believed the unspoken rules were unchangeable rules.

Consider how to offer grace to that person/persons and write down your thoughts:

Samaritan Woman

Life for the Samaritan woman would have been specific regarding her rights and duties as a woman. In her agrarian culture, survival was paramount and everyone had responsibilities. Everyone worked hard. One of her duties would have been to carry the water for the household.

Jesus saw the woman she was intended to be; the Proverbs 31 woman. His first response to her speaks of the "gift" of life God had for her. Jesus also knew her emotions could easily get in the way, so he gently guided her to a place of understanding through love.

The Proverbs 31 woman could be trusted and she offered trust to others. Jesus desired much more for the Samaritan woman than she desired for herself. She was only trying to survive. Jesus wanted her to experience authentic trust. Read Proverbs 3:5-6. What does this tell us about how trust comes to us? Where was the Samaritan woman in the process of trust?

The woman found Jesus' response about "living water" confusing and she asked him a series of problems and questions.

Jesus continued to guide the woman back to the answer that would offer the woman life. Jesus and the woman were not talking about the same issue. The woman wanted physical water because she reasoned her thirst would be forever quenched and she would never have to come to the well again. The woman saw the exterior issue at hand and she was looking for a quick way to resolve her emotions. Jesus loved her and knew she needed to cope with her emotions, and he also knew she first needed a spiritual change in her life.

Name a time in your life when God has given you answers to solve life's problems. How did God guide you?

List the problems and questions the woman identified in John 4:11-12.

Consider your emotions, preconceived expectations from your culture, and your past experiences that can carry hidden emotions. How would those effect a conversation with Jesus?

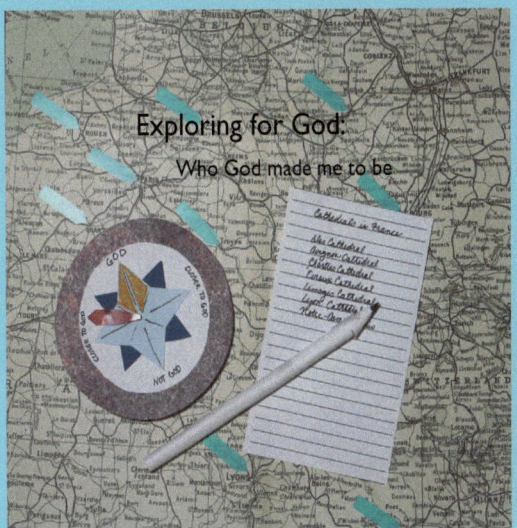

Exploring for God:
Who God made me to be

UNIT 1
EXPLORING WHO GOD
MADE ME TO BE

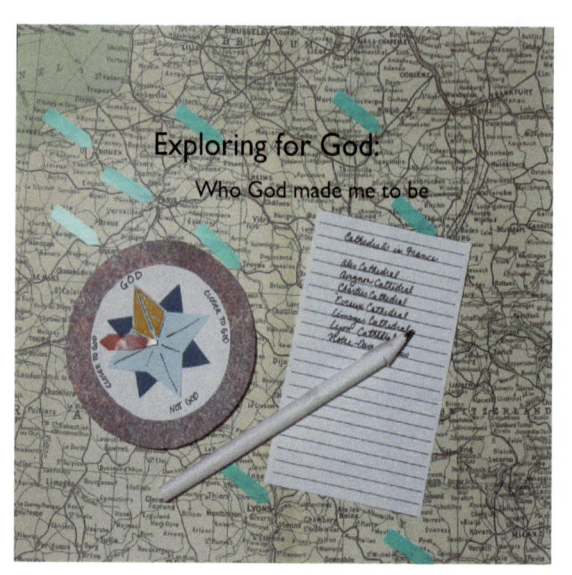

CHAPTER 2
SPIRITUAL

WOMAN OF VALOR
THE WOMAN AT THE WELL

Proverbs 31:30

שֶׁ֣קֶר הַ֭חֵן וְהֶ֣בֶל הַיֹּ֑פִי אִשָּׁ֥ה יִרְאַת־יְ֝הוָ֗ה הִ֣יא תִתְהַלָּֽל׃

The verse translates: deceitful charm vane beauty; the woman who fears The Lord is praised.

John 4:16-26 "Go and get your husband," Jesus told her.

"I don't have a husband," the woman replied.

Jesus said, "You're right! You don't have a husband— for you have had five husbands, and you aren't even married to the man you're living with now. You certainly spoke the truth!" "Sir," the woman said, "you must be a prophet. So tell me, why is it that you Jews insist that Jerusalem is the only place of worship, while we Samaritans claim it is here at Mount Gerizim, where our ancestors worshiped?" Jesus replied, "Believe me, dear woman, the time is coming when it will no longer matter whether you worship the Father on this mountain or in Jerusalem. You Samaritans know very little about the one you worship, while we Jews know all about him, for salvation comes through the Jews. But the time is coming—indeed it's here now—when true worshipers will worship the Father in spirit and in truth. The Father is looking for those who will worship him that way. For God is Spirit, so those who worship him must worship in spirit and in truth." The woman said, "I know the Messiah is coming—the one who is called Christ. When he comes, he will explain everything to us." Then Jesus told her, "I Am the Messiah!"

Jesus turns attention to the Samaritan Woman's personal life.

He gets right to the heart of the matter when he asks her:

'where is your husband?'

Notes:

LET'S GET PERSONAL

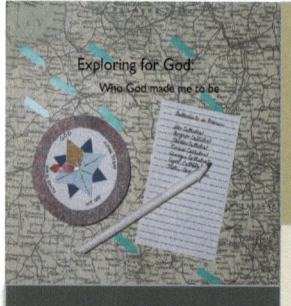

JOURNAL

You are in the airport waiting to get on the plane. Your nerves are a little on edge from the rush to get here and a difficult security check-in. While you wait for the boarding call a man from Africa comes over and starts talking to you. You really want to be left alone, but he is kind and gentle so you don't excuse yourself. While he talks you wonder why he is talking to you. It's unusual for an African man to approach an American woman he has not been introduced to. What do you think about the man? Do you feel safe? Are you guarded?

After a while the conversation turns to personal matters. That's when you get uncomfortable and you change the subject. He seems to change it back and every word he utters pierces your heart but at the same time it feels warm and comforting. You've never done this before but you open up to him; you trust him. He doesn't criticize or even counsel. With his loving words he draws you closer to him.

Suddenly the announcement comes in over the loud speaker that they are boarding the plane. You start to look for your ticket and check your luggage. Then you remember the man, your new friend and he is gone. Sadness sweeps over you yet you still feel warm and loved from the time you had together. As you get up to board the plane you hear his voice saying, "I'm always here...you only need to ask and you will receive."

His love, that same restoring love poured through you and in an instant you know your life will never be the same again.

As you board the plane you realize that even though your meeting was unusual and unexpected you are grateful that the man sought you out and took tIme to love you!

INTENT

Jesus was not condemning or criticizing the woman. He was loving the woman today and was loving the woman he knew she could be. Jesus saw everything God wanted for her! The same is true for you. God sees you as the person he created you to be. What is Jesus telling you he wants for you?

The Real Deal

The woman needed to know Jesus was authentic...the real deal sent from God. The Samaritan woman responded by shifting the conversation away from her personal life to a discussion about worship. What was the woman thinking?

The Winds of Change

Jesus always has the bigger picture in mind for us. Jesus wanted to reach the woman spiritually. The woman wanted to talk about why the Jews and Samaritans worship differently while Jesus directed her to the changes that were about to happen. He was telling her everything is about to change. Jesus was preparing her for her new life ahead. Jesus always prepares us when we receive what he has for us.

The Promised One

The Samaritan woman spoke of the promised Messiah and Jesus responded by saying, "I AM" the one.

Who is the 'I AM'?

Prophet

The Samaritan woman knew he was a prophet and so she listened intently to what Jesus said. That also explains why she was making the connection about the coming Messiah.

I AM PROMISE PROPHET SAVIOR

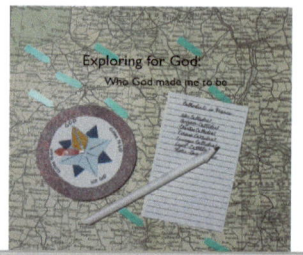

In John 4:25-26 the prophet she spoke of would have been a prophet like Moses. By using the words "I AM" Jesus was telling her he was the one Moses spoke TO.

Spiritual Practice:

Take 20 minutes (you can set a timer if you want) and experience the "I AM". Write down your thoughts immediately after your time together. Post your thoughts below to serve as a reminder of your time throughout the day.

Jesus was not making racial comments when he spoke of the Jews and Samaritans. Jesus was clearly telling the woman God chose the nation of Israel to take the message of salvation and restoration to the world.

EXPERIENCE

Unit 1
Exploring Who God Made Me to Be

Chapter 3

Relational and Spiritual

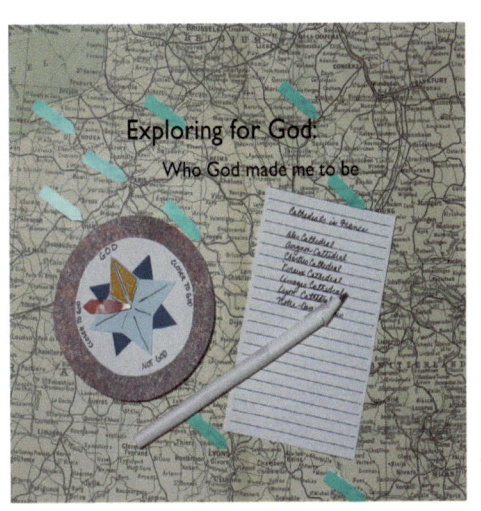

Woman of Valor
The Woman at the Well

John 4:27-42:

Just then his disciples came back. They were shocked to find him talking to a woman, but none of them had the nerve to ask, "What do you want with her?" or "Why are you talking to her?" The woman left her water jar beside the well and ran back to the village, telling everyone, "Come and see a man who told me everything I ever did! Could he possibly be the Messiah?" So the people came streaming from the village to see him. Meanwhile, the disciples were urging Jesus, "Rabbi, eat something." But Jesus replied, "I have a kind of food you know nothing about." "Did someone bring him food while we were gone?" the disciples asked each other. Then Jesus explained: "My nourishment comes from doing the will of God, who sent me, and from finishing his work. You know the saying, 'Four months between planting and harvest.' But I say, wake up and look around. The fields are already ripe for harvest. The harvesters are paid good wages, and the fruit they harvest is people brought to eternal life. What joy awaits both the planter and the harvester alike! You know the saying, 'One plants and another harvests.' And it's true. I sent you to harvest where you didn't plant; others had already done the work, and now you will get to gather the harvest." Many Samaritans from the village believed in Jesus because the woman had said, "He told me everything I ever did!" When they came out to see him, they begged him to stay in their village. So he stayed for two days, long enough for many more to hear his message and believe. Then they said to the woman, "Now we believe, not just because of what you told us, but because we have heard him ourselves. Now we know that he is indeed the Savior of the world." (John 4:27-42 NLT)

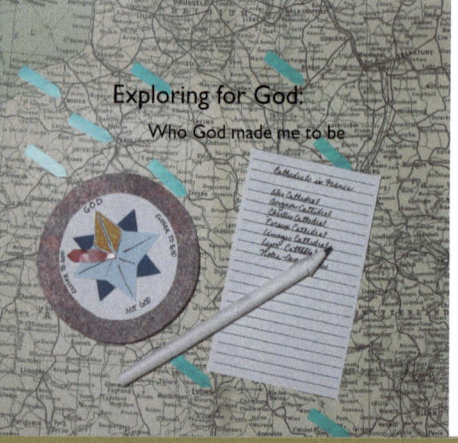

Exploring for God: Who God made me to be

Proverbs 31:12 The woman did good and not harm all the days of her life.

גְּמָלַתְהוּ טוֹב וְלֹא־רָע כֹּל יְמֵי חַיֶּיהָ:

Translated: She did good (Tov) not evil all days of her life.

JESUS LOVES...

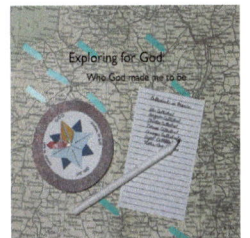

The disciples came back and found Jesus talking to the Samaritan woman. They were shocked at his behavior but no-one said anything.

They wanted to remind Jesus that he should not speak with her...that it was unacceptable for a Jewish man to speak with a Samaritan woman.

Restoration Box: Jesus was telling the disciples that we are restored (fed) by doing the will of God. It's funny...we seem to think of it as 'having' to do the will of God instead of being restored by doing God's will in our lives. We automatically assume we are making great sacrifices and should be given some sort of a medal. Instead, we need to realize by doing God's will we can relax. He will give us all we need to fulfill our purpose. By doing that we are FILLED. John 10:10 says, "The thief's purpose is to steal and kill and destroy. My purpose is to give them a rich and satisfying life."

Our culture tells us we have to work hard, make great sacrifices and maybe then we will be acceptable. We are also led to believe we need to please others. Jesus says he wants to GIVE life to us. We do not have to work to find our purpose or make great sacrifices. When we pray and wait for God to bring His good purpose to us we are satisfied IN him. The sacrifice becomes joy IN him. We are acceptable to him as we are. We do not need to please anyone outside of God.

The woman ran to town to tell everyone about Jesus. Interestingly enough, she understood the big picture and because she had been transformed she acted on her desire to 'go and tell'.

Go and Tell: It's been my experience that when people hear the word "evangelism" they start to tighten up and immediately wonder what that means. Jesus is saying to the disciples that others who came before have sown the seed and watered it and now it is ready for harvest. They were called to harvest the crop.

Today there are times we are called to sow the seed by loving others who do not know the truth about Jesus. Others are called to water the seed by loving them and encouraging them daily. Still others are called to harvest the fully grown seed by leading them to a point where they can accept God's love and grace. Knowing the stage of the seed is a matter of discernment and listening to the Spirit.

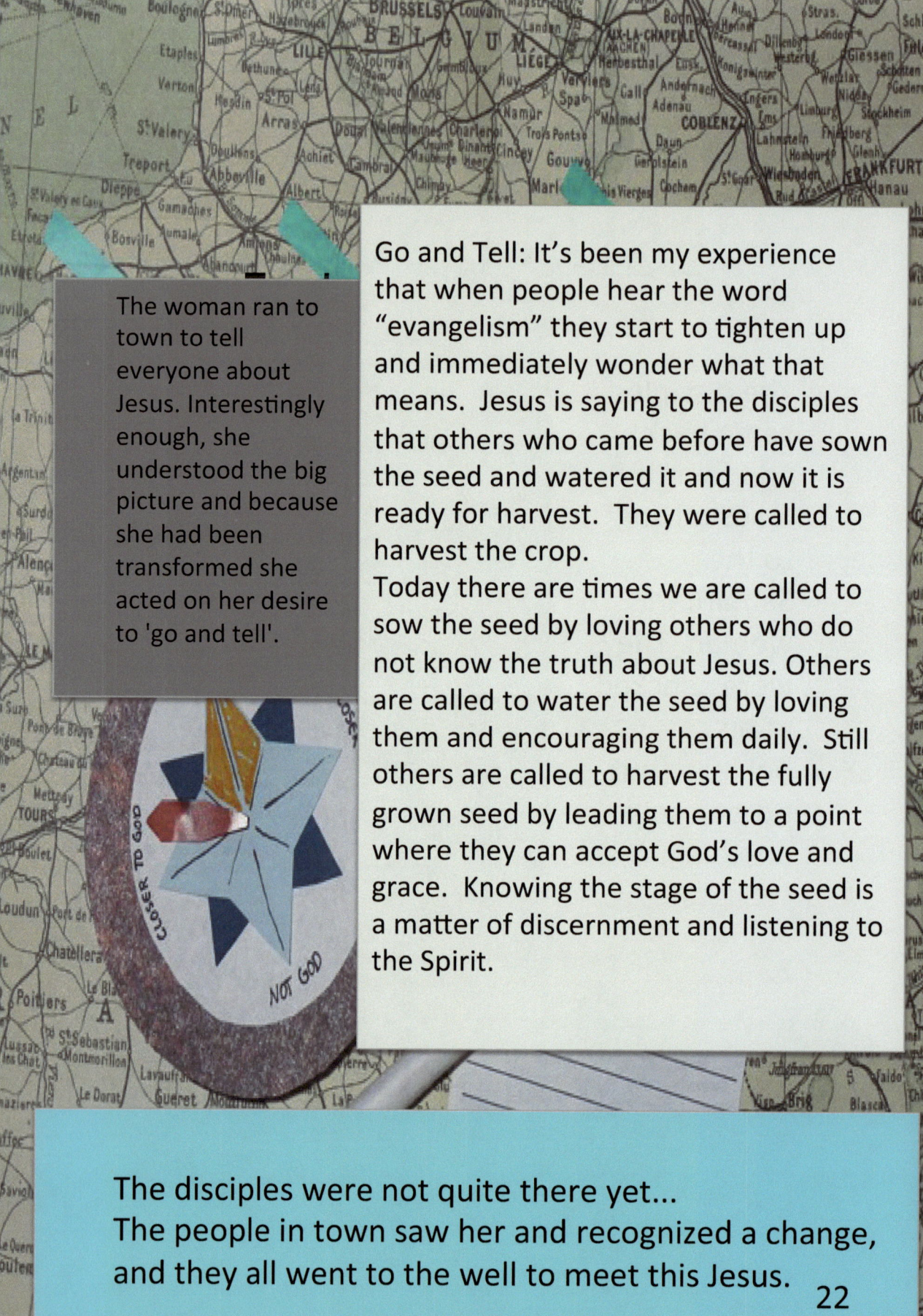

The disciples were not quite there yet...
The people in town saw her and recognized a change, and they all went to the well to meet this Jesus.

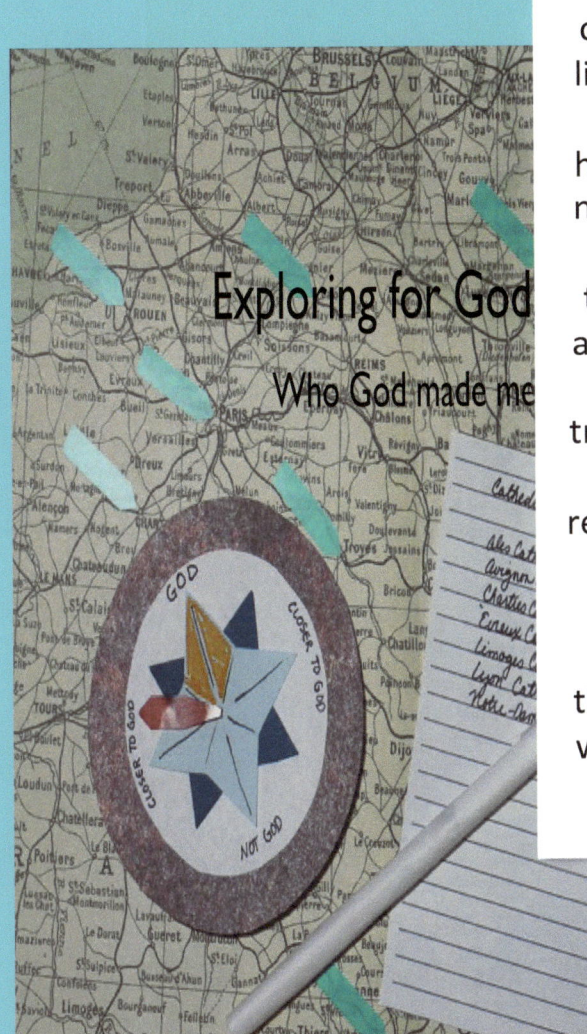

The Samaritan woman had been silent and had most likely separated herself from others in the village because of her past life. Even though it is quite possible that she had been 'put out' by several husbands and being with many men was not her choice, she still would have been blamed and shunned. Jesus knew the truth about her past. He knew her pain and sorrow. Jesus loved her and saw her as she could be. Because Jesus was truthful and loving with her, she was able to put away her past and receive restoration in God. When the woman ran to town to tell everyone about Jesus 'Messiah', they would have seen the transformation. Her life spoke eons to them and they too, came to receive. The woman was listening and followed God's will for her life. As a result, she was satisfied and full in Christ.

Many were restored to God's love that day because Jesus loved the Samaritan woman, restored her emotionally, transformed her spiritually, and healed her relationally.
She was whole. Holy in Christ. Eternal. Never the same again.

The wise woman in Proverbs 31:12 did good all the days of her life. She wasn't thinking of herself but was seeking God's will. When Jesus first met the Samaritan woman she was turned inward and was focused on her own pain of rejection. After she met Jesus and was touched by his love, she was healed and was able to turn outward. Because of Jesus' love she was able to offer goodness and compassion to the people in the village.

Experience

Exploring for God:

Who God made me to be

Memorize Psalm 23:1 (NLT); "The Lord is my Shepherd, I have everything I need." Listen to the Spirit for what he has for you. Write down what you hear and receive throughout the day. With God, giving isn't a matter of scarcity…it's a matter of abundance. As often as you ask, God provides. You cannot ask too much or too often for his love and the gift of his Spirit.

UNIT II CHAPTERS 4 – 7
EXPLORING MY PERSONAL SPACE

THE WOMAN AT THE WELL

WOMAN OF VALOR

PROVERBS 31:25-26
SHE IS CLOTHED WITH STRENGTH AND DIGNITY, AND SHE LAUGHS WITHOUT FEAR OF THE FUTURE. WHEN SHE SPEAKS, HER WORDS ARE WISE, AND SHE GIVES INSTRUCTIONS WITH KINDNESS. (NLT)

UNIT II
EXPLORING MY PERSONAL SPACE

CHAPTER 4
CHARACTER

WOMAN OF VALOR
THE WOMAN AT THE WELL

Proverbs 31:25-26
Strength and dignity are her clothing, and she laughs at the time to come.

She opens her mouth with wisdom, and the teaching of kindness is on her tongue.

עֹז־וְהָדָר לְבוּשָׁהּ וַתִּשְׂחַק לְיוֹם אַחֲרוֹן׃
פִּיהָ פָּתְחָה בְחָכְמָה וְתוֹרַת־חֶסֶד עַל־לְשׁוֹנָהּ׃

Luke 1:28-38
Gabriel appeared to her and said, "Greetings, favored woman! The Lord is with you!" Confused and disturbed, Mary tried to think what the angel could mean. "Don't be afraid, Mary,"

A glowing (rather large) angel is standing before me but I'm not afraid! Mary's response seems perfectly normal to me...

"the angel told her, "for you have found favor with God! You will conceive and give birth to a son, and you will name him Jesus. He will be very great and will be called the Son of the Most High. The Lord God will give him the throne of his ancestor David. And he will reign over Israel forever; his Kingdom will never end!"

Now consider that Mary was a young woman and had not 'known' a man. The angels message that she was going to have a child would certainly be confusing. When you add the rest of the message it is mind-blowing! Not only will this child be special, he will be the Son of God who will reign forever! Okay, so wait...I don't recall that this has been done before (or since!).

Mary asked the angel, "But how can this happen? I am a virgin." The angel replied, "The Holy Spirit will come upon you, and the power of the Most High will overshadow you. So the baby to be born will be holy, and he will be called the Son of God. What's more, your relative Elizabeth has become pregnant in her old age! People used to say she was barren, but she has conceived a son and is now in her sixth month.

Mary's question had merit. So, how is this gonna happen? Put yourself in Mary's shoes. You are a young virgin and one day out of the blue an angel appears and tells you that you are going to have a baby and he will be holy. What exactly does that mean? The best news you get is that someone you know is having a baby, too. Since you will be shamed and possibly shunned you know you have someplace to go so you can process all of this.

...and Mary heads off to visit Elizabeth.

The other problem is that somehow you have to explain this to the man your parents promised you to. You wonder where to begin? You know that if you tell him an angel visited you and told you that you were going to be the mother of God he will think you're crazy!

You also have to tell your parents. They will probably be totally upset and think you are lying. They gave their word to the man they promised you to, that you've not been with a man and now it totally looks like they lied, too. They are going to be so upset. Honestly, who can blame them? It is a really far out story!

MARY RESPONDED, "I AM THE LORD'S SERVANT. MAY EVERYTHING YOU HAVE SAID ABOUT ME COME TRUE." AND THEN THE ANGEL LEFT HER. (LUKE 1:28-36, 38 NLT)

Despite the obstacles Mary faced, she immediately surrendered to God's will.

What is clear is that Mary was a woman who trusted God and relied on His strength. Even in the face of incredible problems that seem to have no solution she relied on God's strength. God honored her when he chose her to be Mother of God because she possessed dignity of character even in the most difficult circumstances. Mary relied on God's strength. She was an honored woman.

And Mary's response? She praised God!

Elizabeth recognized the honor God gave Mary: Luke 1:43-45, "Why am I so honored, that the mother of my Lord should visit me? When I heard your greeting, the baby in my womb jumped for joy. You are blessed because you believed that the Lord would do what he said." (NLT)

UNIT II

CHAPTER 5

EXPLORING YOUR
PERSONAL SPACE

GIFTS

WOMAN OF VALOR

Proverbs 31:25b she laughs at the time to come

The Hebrew word: שָׂחַק

Pronounced sachaq means to laugh, smile, or to rejoice.

THE GIFT OF FAITH

Mary rejoiced in the future.

Mary pondered...

Luke 2:19, when she gave birth to a son far away from family and home in a strange city, she rejoiced.

When she had to pack up her son and go to Egypt to escape King Herod's wrath, she rejoiced.

Mary pondered...

When she sought her twelve year old son and found him teaching in the Temple, she rejoiced.

AND SHE TREASURED...

LUKE 2:51B

Do you ponder with God?

Sit with the Spirit and ask questions?

Listen for the movement of the Spirit?

Wait on God...

When she asked him to turn the water into wine, she rejoiced.

When she visited him and asked to see him, she shed a tear because she missed her first-born son and rejoiced when he did not come out.

When she saw him heal, and restore, she rejoiced.

> Do you rejoice?
> Mary rejoiced knowing that God was in charge.
> She knew Jesus had a plan and was on track with that plan.
> Even when times were difficult she knew God was taking care of everything.
> In light of that, do you rejoice knowing God has everything taken care of?

When he walked to road to Gethsemane, she wept and she rejoiced.

When she stood at the foot of the cross, her heart broke, and she rejoiced.

She knew he was fully man. She knew he was fully God.

She knew he was Messiah.

She knew he was Son.

She knew because God told her.

He was faithful and gave her faith.

Mary's moment, the moment she had waited for came the morning of the third day after his death. She believed he was sent to save and when she saw the empty tomb she knew. She knew God had a plan and that even though there was pain and heartache and sweat and tears, God's plan would come to pass.

She never **doubted** it for a minute.

God said it…

It was true.

> **What are Spiritual Gifts? Exactly what it sounds like. A "gift" from the Spirit. Spiritual gifts are a gift from God that we need spiritually to accomplish God's purpose. God gives us exactly what we need. He also gives us passion to complete the task.**

Gifts of the Spirit: I Corinthians 12:4-11; Ephesians 4:7-13; I Peter 4:10; and Romans 12:6-8.

List of gifts include:

Experience YOUR Gifts!

Take a spiritual gifts test

List your gifts:

and ponder...

UNIT II

CHAPTER 6

WISE

BEING WHO GOD CREATED YOU TO BE

WOMAN OF VALOR
MARY, MOTHER OF JESUS

Mary's response to the news that she would conceive the child of God was filled with acceptance, surrender, and praise.

The Magnificat: Mary's Song of Praise
Mary responded,
"Oh, how my soul praises the Lord.
 How my spirit rejoices in God my Savior!
For he took notice of his lowly servant girl,
 and from now on all generations will call me blessed.
For the Mighty One is holy,
 and he has done great things for me.
He shows mercy from generation to generation
 to all who fear him.
His mighty arm has done tremendous things!
 He has scattered the proud and haughty ones.
He has brought down princes from their thrones
 and exalted the humble.
He has filled the hungry with good things
 and sent the rich away with empty hands.
He has helped his servant Israel
 and remembered to be merciful.
For he made this promise to our ancestors,
 to Abraham and his children forever." (NLT)

PROVERBS 31:26A

She opens her mouth with wisdom.

The structure of Hebrew poetry often includes parallelism. Notice the parallel structure of the first two lines. Those are a precursor to the remainder of the song. Each line after that could easily begin with "For..." or "Because" and those statements all point back to the first two lines.

In verse 50 Mary quotes Psalm 103:17 emphasizing God's faithfulness. Mary also emphasizes Hebrew Old Testament themes of God raising up the humble and lowering the proud. See Proverbs 3:34 and Isaiah 2:11-12.

In the song, Mary quotes parts of Psalm 33:1, Psalm 47:1, Psalm 95:2, and Psalm 149:1-5.

Psalm 107:9 speaks of God's mercy to those in need. Hebrew scripture was spoken and memorized. The last part of The Shema (Deuteronomy 6:4-9) says, "Tie them as symbols on your hands and bind them on your foreheads. Write them on the door frames of your houses and your gates." Mary's song was an extension of her Jewish heritage.

Mary knew of God's promise to Abraham and that Israel was chosen to tell the nations of God's love and justice. There are similarities of themes found in Isaiah 42 thru 49 and Matthew 12:15-18. YHWH (YAHWEH) is a God of mercy and justice and Mary's song reminds us of God's wiseman.
Most likely she had heard those spoken throughout her childhood.

The Shema (Deuteronomy 6:4-9) says in verses 6-7, "These commandments that I give you today are to be on your hearts. Impress them on your children. Talk about them when you sit at home and when you walk along the road, when you lie down and when you get up."

Finally, Mary's song of praise has similarities to Hannah's song of praise in 1 Samuel 2:1-10. Both women knew their promised child would be a change agent for God. Certainly Samuel was God's man of the hour and Jesus WAS the promised Messiah the prophets spoke of in scripture!

Mary humbly spoke wisdom and the truth of God's justice and mercy.
Mary's song, full of praise for his promise fulfilled to Israel.

Experience: Write your own magnificat to God. Tell God what you praise Him for and express your love in return.

UNIT II

CHAPTER 7

THROUGH ADVERSITY

WOMAN OF VALOR
MARY, MOTHER OF JESUS

In Luke 2:35 (RSV) Simeon told Mary what was to come:

"Behold, this child is set for the fall and rising of many in Israel, and for a sign that is spoken against (and a sword will pierce through your soul also), that thoughts out of many hearts will be revealed."

PROVERBS 31:26B
KINDNESS IS ON HER TONGUE

In Luke 2:19 and Luke 2:51 we learn a great deal about Mary's character. After the shepherds came to see the Christ child, Mary "treasured up all these things and pondered them in her heart." Then when Mary and Joseph found Jesus in the Temple when he was twelve years old, they were astonished. Here was their boy sitting with the teachers in the Temple courts! And as they went to Nazareth "his mother treasured all these things in her heart.

It was Mary's boy who turned the water to wine. He healed the sick.
Mary's boy taught to thousands on the hillsides and expelled demons from tormented souls.
Her boy showed compassion to children and adulterous women. No one else even saw those souls...her son lifted them up and transformed them.
Mary's oldest born raised Lazarus from the dead and entered Jerusalem riding on a donkey to the shouts of 'Hosanna'!
Her boy had an amazing week of teaching in Jerusalem, but at the same time Mary noticed the Pharisees were watching closely and were whispering among themselves.
She wondered what they were talking about.

On Thursday night Jesus and the twelve had a peaceful night of fellowship
before they went to the garden to pray.
Then in an instant everything changed.
Mary's boy was arrested.
Beaten.
Tried.
Convicted.
Sent to be crucified.
They spit on him.
Mary's son had to carry his own cross up the hill and the blood from his body left a trail.
They hammered nails in his hands and feet and Mary felt every blow.
They hung him on a tree fashioned in the shape of a cross.
They took his clothes so he would die in shame.
His blood covered the ground…it was everywhere.

Then her boy forgave them.
He remembered her and made sure she would be cared for.
Mary's boy gave up his spirit.
He died on the cross that day.
They pierced his side to make sure he was dead.
Mary's soul was pierced that day.

They laid her boy in a tomb.
The hope of Israel was in the tomb.

The hope of the world was dead.

Even though Mary suffered great adversity she bore her sorrows with loving kindness and trust in God. Mary held in her heart everything that happened and had been foretold. She treasured those things in her pierced heart.

She wondered what her boy meant when he said, "Destroy this Temple, and in three days I will raise it up." Was did God have planned?

All of this WAS for a reason!

After the Sabbath was over Mary went to bed without eating. She had hardly slept since they took her boy away. Finally, sometime during the early hours on Sunday morning Mary dropped off to sleep. When she awoke on Sunday she felt different. A sense of anticipation filled the room. The stabbing pain in her heart was gone. For the first time in three days she could breathe. She remembered that her boy died but she no longer felt his death.

Suddenly she heard shouts from outside. Someone was running and yelling. She couldn't quite make it out, but someone was shouting something about "risen" or "rise up". Was she dreaming? No. She was awake.

Mary got up and went outside to find out what was going on. It didn't take long to figure out that they were talking about her boy Jesus. They were saying, "He is risen"!

Mary wondered, is it true? The others were saying that Mary Magdalene and the other women went to the tomb. They didn't wake her because she hadn't slept in days.

Now, she needed to find Mary Magdalene. She started down the walkway and she heard Mary yelling her name... "Mother Mary, Mother Mary!"

She was breathless but through her breath and with tears streaming down her cheeks she shouted, "He is risen! Mother Mary, Jesus is risen! I saw him and talked to him!"

Risen.

He is alive.

My boy is alive...

'That's my boy' thought Mary as she chuckled to herself.

That's my boy...Oh, that's what three days meant!

She knew all along that the Father had a plan, and what a plan it was!

My son, God's son, is RISEN from the dead!

Experience: meditate on what it would have been like to be there when they found the empty tomb. Put yourself inside the tomb touching the burial clothes.

What do you feel?

See?

Think?

UNIT III CHAPTER 8 & 9

EXPLORING YOUR LIVING SPACE

WOMAN OF VALOR
MARY AND MARTHA

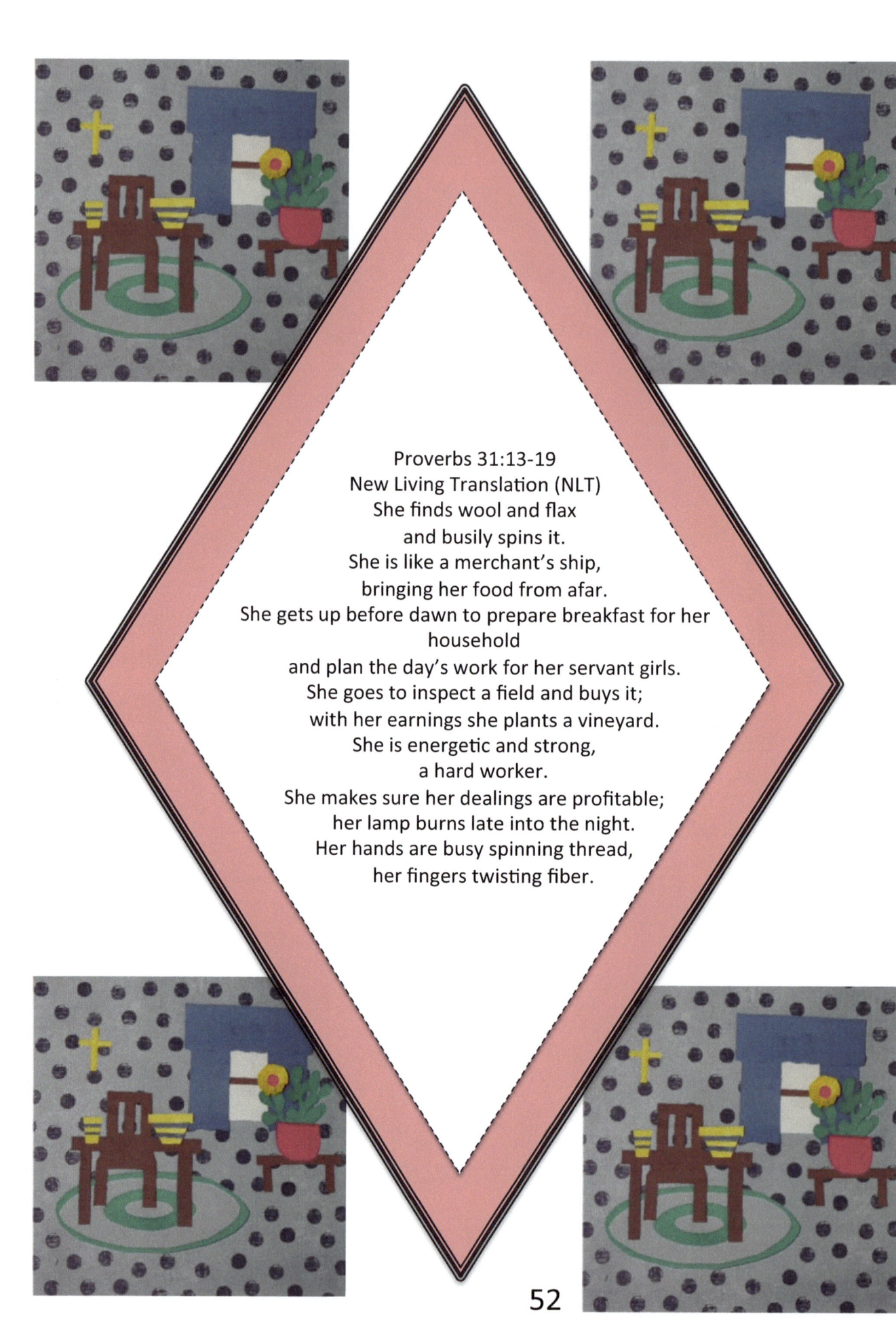

Proverbs 31:13-19
New Living Translation (NLT)
She finds wool and flax
and busily spins it.
She is like a merchant's ship,
bringing her food from afar.
She gets up before dawn to prepare breakfast for her household
and plan the day's work for her servant girls.
She goes to inspect a field and buys it;
with her earnings she plants a vineyard.
She is energetic and strong,
a hard worker.
She makes sure her dealings are profitable;
her lamp burns late into the night.
Her hands are busy spinning thread,
her fingers twisting fiber.

UNIT III

CHAPTER 8

EXPLORING YOUR LIVING SPACE

YOUR SPACE

WOMAN OF VALOR
MARTHA AND MARY

Luke 10:38-42

As Jesus and the disciples continued on their way to Jerusalem, they came to a certain village where a woman named Martha welcomed him into her home. Her sister, Mary, sat at the Lord's feet, listening to what he taught. But Martha was distracted by the big dinner she was preparing. She came to Jesus and said, "Lord, doesn't it seem unfair to you that my sister just sits here while I do all the work? Tell her to come and help me." But the Lord said to her, "My dear Martha, you are worried and upset over all these details! There is only one thing worth being concerned about. Mary has discovered it, and it will not be taken away from her." (NLT)

Proverbs 31:13-16
She finds wool and flax
    and busily spins it.
She is like a merchant's ship,
    bringing her food from afar.
She gets up before dawn to prepare breakfast for her household
    and plan the day's work for her servant girls.
She goes to inspect a field and buys it;
    with her earnings she plants a vineyard.

Both sisters learn from Jesus:
This was more about Jesus making a statement about what Mary was doing right than what Martha was doing wrong.

VALUE

Jesus was telling everyone there it was alright for Mary to sit at his feet, be a follower, a disciple. In her culture it would have been highly unusual for Mary to have the right to sit with Jesus and the other disciples.

Jesus came to give everyone value. In Matthew 10:14. Jesus made it clear that the children could come and sit at his feet (or on his lap).

Rabbi Jesus was saying to them, 'come and sit with me.'

Jesus validated Mary and He was also telling Martha that she didn't have to be confined to the kitchen. Jesus was setting Martha free as well.

While everyone had work to do and everyone rose early and often worked until late, Jesus wanted Mary and Martha to know it was okay to set aside time throughout their day to talk to him.

The lesson from Proverbs reminding us that we need to stay active, lovingly utilizing our gifts for our families and the lesson from Jesus telling women they are also disciples are both pertinent to women today. The Proverbs 31 woman was a shrewd business woman. The same is true today. When we purchase clothing for ourselves or our loved ones (department store or garage sale), don't we look it over and feel the fabric? Don't we look at the colors? Additionally, Jesus was telling the women they have a special place in the kingdom. Jesus reminded Martha she had the right to take time from serving and sit at his feet and rest. While serving is important, so is rest.

Mary and Martha did many of those same tasks but Jesus was telling them as women they were disciples as well. Today, women work inside and outside the home providing for needs, but Jesus wants us to remember to take time to sit at his feet. We cannot be so busy that we forget to sit at his feet!

PSALM 37:7
EXODUS 14:14
PSALM 46:10
ECC. 5:1
MATTHEW 6:6
MATTHEW 21:22
MATTHEW 6:9
MATTHEW 14:23
MATTHEW 26:39
MATTHEW 26:41-44
MARK 1:35
MARK 6:46
MARK 9:29
MARK 11:25
LUKE 3:21
MATTHEW 19:13

Experience: Clearly prayer (talking to God) is an important component to our spiritual growth and development. Take time to talk to Jesus today, telling him you love him.

UNIT III

CHAPTER 9

EXPLORING YOUR
LIVING SPACE:
EASY CHANGES

WOMAN OF VALOR
MARTHA AND MARY

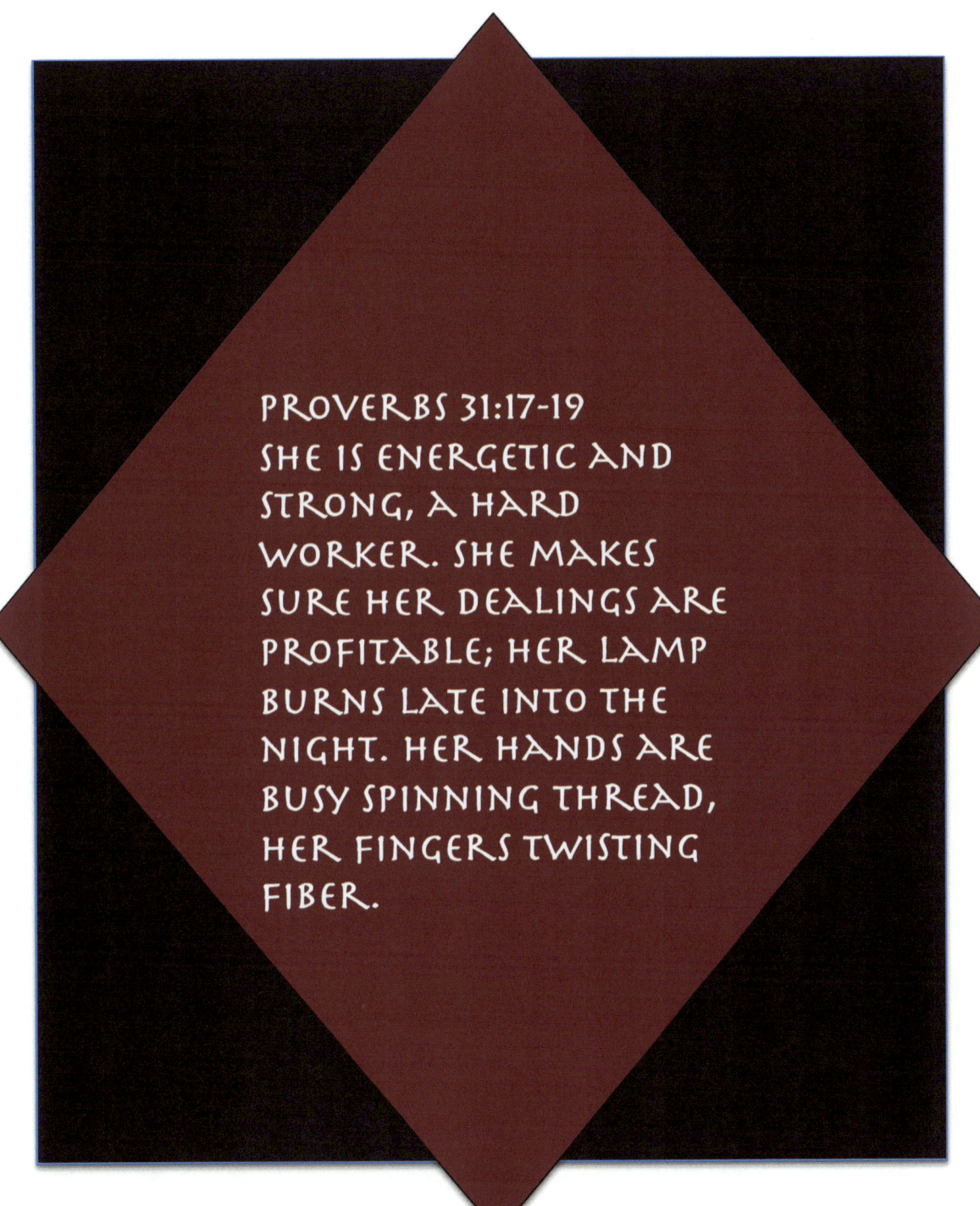

PROVERBS 31:17-19
SHE IS ENERGETIC AND STRONG, A HARD WORKER. SHE MAKES SURE HER DEALINGS ARE PROFITABLE; HER LAMP BURNS LATE INTO THE NIGHT. HER HANDS ARE BUSY SPINNING THREAD, HER FINGERS TWISTING FIBER.

Habits are part of our lives and changes to routines and patterns do not come easy. That's why when we make emotional or spiritual changes (or other changes) we grieve the loss of the familiar. When making changes, give yourself grace and remind yourself you are okay and that it's normal to miss your old way of doing things.

All of that is why when making changes to your life it's important to rely on God and to stay close to him. Jesus will help you with the transformation!

The Proverbs 31 poem gives the reader the sense of an energetic woman. She is not lazy and she makes wise decisions. This wise woman spends evenings spinning thread well into the night and I imagine while she spins she sings to the Lord her lovely song of praise.

Transforming Restoration

Mary and Martha AFTER Lazarus' Resurrection

John 12:1-8 "Six days before the Passover celebration began, Jesus arrived in Bethany, the home of Lazarus—the man he had raised from the dead. A dinner was prepared in Jesus' honor. Martha served, and Lazarus was among those who ate with him. Then Mary took a twelve-ounce jar of expensive perfume made from essence of nard, and she anointed Jesus' feet with it, wiping his feet with her hair. The house was filled with the fragrance. But Judas Iscariot, the disciple who would soon betray him, said, "That perfume was worth a year's wages. It should have been sold and the money given to the poor." Not that he cared for the poor—he was a thief, and since he was in charge of the disciples' money, he often stole some for himself. Jesus replied, "Leave her alone. She did this in preparation for my burial. You will always have the poor among you, but you will not always have me." (NLT)

Martha's Story: Mary and I are so blessed by Jesus! Our brother Lazarus has been raised from the dead and we planned a banquet in Jesus' honor. While we have maidens who could serve, I choose the honor of serving Jesus myself. I do so love serving others!

Peace fills the room...

Mary's Story: After the lavish meal, I opened an expensive jar of perfume that I had been saving for such a special occasion as this. As soon as I removed the lid from the jar the smell flooded the room with a rich lavish scent. I took down my hair and knelt at the feet of Jesus to anoint his tired feet. As I soothed his tired feet I pondered the miles he walks daily in order to heal the sick, encourage the downtrodden, and teach of God's precious love. I wiped Jesus' feet with my hair and sat at his feet taking time to listen to Jesus speak. I hold that precious memory in my heart and will remember the shared love forever!

Judas turns the conversation to worldly matters by reminding everyone of the cost of the perfume. He suggests it should have been used for other purposes, like feeding the poor. Is Mary unsure about her gift? Did she do something wrong? I knew her gift was meant to honor her Lord, and it was not meant for harm.

Jesus always seemed to see things others don't see, like Judas' heart, and Jesus tells him to leave Mary alone. Then, Jesus says something puzzling. He tells Judas it was meant in preparation for his burial. I wondered what that meant. Why would Jesus be planning his burial now? He also said we wouldn't always have him here. I knew he would travel to see others and I thought perhaps that was what he meant.

Still, I couldn't imagine life without Jesus. Everywhere he went he brought love and such peace! I thought that Jesus was unlike anyone I'd ever known. He gives and gives and we so desperately need what he offers!

After the maidens have the kitchen picked up and put back in order, I retire to my spinning in the corner of the room, just far enough away to hear Jesus talk. As I spin thread, the sound of Jesus' voice floods the room with peace. What a glorious night this has been! I am so grateful for the presence of Jesus, our Lord!

Transformation

Martha was transformed from a hurried server when she first met Jesus to a woman who realized that serving others was a gift that brought her great joy!
She also learned it was alright to take time to sit at Jesus' feet and in doing so she was transformed from slave to servant.

Mary was learning as well that it really was safe to offer gifts of love. Her intention of honoring Jesus with an expensive bottle of perfume pleased Jesus. The desire of Mary's heart was not to please everyone; she wanted to do what pleased her Lord!

Experience

Ask God how he wants to transform you?

_____

_____

_____

_____

_____

_____

UNIT IV CHAPTERS 10 AND 11 EXPLORING COMMUNICATION

WOMAN OF VALOR
THE WOMAN BLEEDING

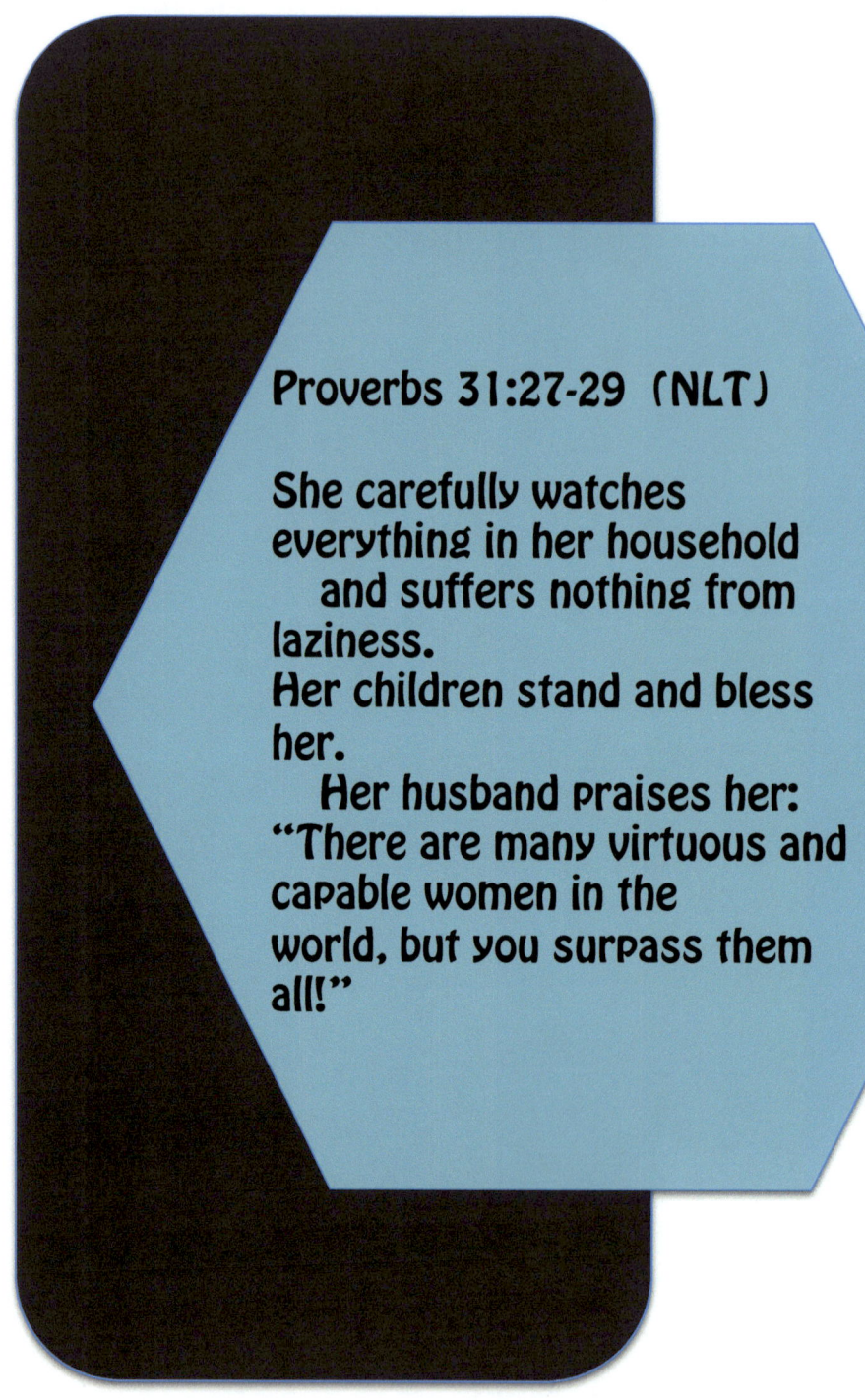

Proverbs 31:27-29 (NLT)

She carefully watches everything in her household
    and suffers nothing from laziness.
Her children stand and bless her.
    Her husband praises her: "There are many virtuous and capable women in the world, but you surpass them all!"

UNIT IV

CHAPTER 10

EXPLORING COMMUNICATION

WOMEN

WOMAN OF VALOR
THE BLEEDING WOMAN WHO TOUCHED THE HEM OF HIS GARMENT

Mark 5:25-34
Jesus went with him (Jarius), and all the people followed, crowding around him. A woman in the crowd had suffered for twelve years with constant bleeding.
She had suffered a great deal from many doctors, and over the years she had spent everything she had to pay them, but she had gotten no better. In fact, she had gotten worse.
She had heard about Jesus, so she came up behind him through the crowd and touched his robe. For she thought to herself, "If I can just touch his robe, I will be healed."
Immediately the bleeding stopped, and she could feel in her body that she had been healed of her terrible condition.
Jesus realized at once that healing power had gone out from him, so he turned around in the crowd and asked, "Who touched my robe?" His disciples said to him, "Look at this crowd pressing around you. How can you ask, 'Who touched me?'" But he kept on looking around to see who had done it.
Then the frightened woman, trembling at the realization of what had happened to her, came and fell to her knees in front of him and told him what she had done. And he said to her, "Daughter, your faith has made you well. Go in peace. Your suffering is over." (NLT)

Proverbs 31:27-28a
She carefully watches everything in her household and suffers nothing from laziness. Her children stand and bless her.

The Woman in Mark 5:24-34 was a desperate woman. She had tried everything to stop the bleeding and nothing had worked. Additionally, when a woman was bleeding she was rendered unclean and no man could touch her lest he become unclean as well. Because of that, if she had a husband he probably would have divorced her. If she was single, she would have been left with no one to care for her.

The Woman who touched the hem of Jesus' garment was timid about approaching him with her need and because she was unclean she should have not been in public. She had very good reasons to be hesitant. First, while it was acceptable for a man to publicly approach another man he didn't know, it was more difficult for a woman but unacceptable for a woman bleeding. Plus, this man was a famous Rabbi! The woman believed so strongly in Jesus that she knew if she could touch any part of him she would be healed. She was correct and she was healed.

The woman believed her communication with Jesus would remain a secret. She never expected Jesus to "feel" the healing power leave his body. When Jesus turned and asked, "Who touched my robe?" the woman became frightened. Suddenly what she thought would be a secret became a public knowledge!

69

When Jesus' disciples began talking among themselves asking 'did you see who touched Jesus?', the woman wanted to run away. She wanted to disappear in the crowd! What would she say to Jesus' disciples if they found out she was the one who touched Jesus? Thankfully, the disciples seemed to think it would be impossible to figure out who touched Jesus because there were so many people I'm the crowd.

Jesus didn't just heal people physically, he always touched base with them spiritually to connect and heal the deepest part of them. Jesus pressed on because he had more for this woman than she had asked for. While Jesus was fully man, he was also fully God and he knew this woman's needs went beyond the bleeding. Jesus wanted to fully restore this woman.

She hoped that would end the discussion. That didn't happen because Jesus knew healing power left his body. He pressed on. He continued to look through the crowd for this person who needed healing.

The woman's story no doubt didn't end here. When she returned to society she most likely would have told everyone of the change, that she met the famous Rabbi, and was healed. She would have told all of the women in her town about her brush with fame. She would also have told the women the details of her illness. Women love details. They can talk for hours about every side and detail of their lives. Jesus made it possible for the woman to have friends again, establish relationships, and to communicate openly with others.

Experience:

When have you been an outcast?

What did it feel like?

If you know of a woman who is in need of comfort and acceptance take time to touch base with her this week. If you don't know of anyone, pray for the outcast women in your city.

What was the result of your prayers?

UNIT IV

CHAPTER 11

EXPLORING
COMMUNICATION
MEN

WOMAN OF VALOR
THE BLEEDING WOMAN WHO TOUCHED
THE HEM OF HIS GARMENT

PROVERBS 31:28B-29: HER HUSBAND PRAISES HER: "THERE ARE MANY VIRTUOUS AND CAPABLE WOMEN IN THE WORLD, BUT YOU SURPASS THEM ALL!" (NLT)

Mark 5:25-34 Jesus went with him (Jarius), and all the people followed, crowding around him. A woman in the crowd had suffered for twelve years with constant bleeding.

She had suffered a great deal from many doctors, and over the years she had spent everything she had to pay them, but she had gotten no better. In fact, she was worse.

She had heard about Jesus, so she came up behind him through the crowd and touched his robe. For she thought to herself, "If I can just touch his robe, I will be healed." Immediately the bleeding stopped, and she could feel in her body that she had been healed of her terrible condition.
Jesus realized at once that healing power had gone out from him, so he turned around in the crowd and asked, "Who touched my robe?" His disciples said to him, "Look at this crowd pressing around you. How can you ask, 'Who touched me?'" But he kept on looking around to see who had done it.

Then the frightened woman, trembling at the realization of what had happened to her, came and fell to her knees in front of him and told him what she had done. And he said to her, "Daughter, your faith has made you well. Go in peace. Your suffering is over." (NLT)

Jesus was on a mission following Jarius to his house to heal his daughter. As Jesus passed through the crowd the woman who had suffered from bleeding for twelve years spotted the Rabbi. Until that moment the woman had lost all hope. She had tried everything but only got worse. The woman had heard about the famous Rabbi who healed people and as she looked at Jesus, hope poured over her. She squeezed through the crowd, knowing she would need to act quickly but she would need to be very quiet. She reached out as he passed and was able to barely touch his robe.

In that instant she felt like her hands were on fire and the sparks moved throughout her body. Jesus suddenly stopped and turned looking at the crowd. The woman became really nervous and she wondered what Jesus doing? Why was he looking around?
At the same time she remembered the wounded area. She felt all warm and wonderfully peaceful. Her whole body radiated with heat. Oh, what a magnificently warm sensation this was! She was elated, joyful, full of peace…healed!

Jesus suddenly stopped and turned looking at the crowd. The woman became really nervous…

A man in the Hebrew culture at the time Jesus was born would have been direct and to the point. The instant Jesus knew that healing power had left his body he asked 'who touched my robe?' It's interesting that he knew exactly what happened. He didn't say 'who touched me'? He specifically said, 'who touched my robe?' Despite the reaction of the disciples Jesus kept looking around to find the wounded person. Clearly, he wanted to touch base with them. Jesus didn't have to look far because once he spotted the frightened woman's face he knew she was the one. She knew it as well and she fell to his feet. Jesus knew the intricacies of talking to this wounded woman. He knew she needed him to heal her fully and because a woman was not supposed to approach a man Jesus knew she needed his tender care. Immediately Jesus forgave her, gave her peace, and flooded her with the reassurance that she would suffer no more.

On the other hand the disciples replied with their heads. As they looked around they surmised they had no way of knowing who touched Jesus. Everyone was touching Jesus in the crowd and there were people everywhere so they immediately surmised it was impossible to find the person. They weren't even looking at faces or hearts. For twelve years she had been treated like she had the plague. She was unable to freely go out in public or touch any man.

> **Jesus communicated love and acceptance to the bleeding woman.**

The Proverbs 31 woman's husband knew the importance of appreciating and praising his wife. She loves him for noticing her! This man communicated that he knew her.

Experience:

Spend time receiving God's healing. Ask the Spirit to show you what it feels like if you've not been aware of a time when God has healed you. Note that healing can come in many ways. It can be physical, but it can also be emotional, spiritual, relational, or psychological. God always heals when we ask but we don't always recognize the manner of healing. As you sit with God be attentive to the Spirit so you can recognize how God is at work. And, as always if you need help just ask the Spirit to help you to SEE.

UNIT V

CHAPTERS 12 & 13

CREATIVE EXPLORATION

WOMAN OF VALOR
MARY MAGDALENE

Proverbs 31:21-24

She has no fear of winter for her household, for everyone has warm clothes. She makes her own bedspreads. She dresses in fine linen and purple gowns. Her husband is well known at the city gates, where he sits with the other civic leaders. She makes belted linen garments and sashes to sell to the merchants. (NLT)

UNIT V

CHAPTER 12

CREATIVE CAPACITIES

WOMAN OF VALOR

MARY MAGDALENE

Luke 8:1-3 "Soon afterward Jesus began a tour of the nearby towns and villages, preaching and announcing the Good News about the Kingdom of God. He took his twelve disciples with him, along with some women who had been cured of evil spirits and diseases. Among them were Mary Magdalene, from whom he had cast out seven demons; Joanna, the wife of Chuza, Herod's business manager; Susanna; and many others who were contributing from their own resources to support Jesus and his disciples." (NLT)

Proverbs 31:21-22

She has no fear of winter for her household,
    for everyone has warm clothes.
She makes her own bedspreads.
    She dresses in fine linen and purple gowns.

There were women who followed Jesus everywhere he went and three were mentioned by name in Luke 8:1-3. Mary Magdalene and the female disciples traveled with him and sat with the other disciples as he taught. The women provided for Jesus and the other disciples. We know from Luke 8 that Mary, Joanna, and Susanna made provisions for all the disciples. Jesus' viewed women as people and treated them as equal souls in God's kingdom. He spoke with women, healed women, ate with women, loved women, and included women as disciples. Despite raised eyebrows and critical comments, Jesus continued to establish close relationships with women.

Luke 8:3 mentions Mary as being one of the women who provided for Jesus and his followers. Provision for Jesus and the disciples would have included daily meals, water, clothing, and shoes. Those were just the basics. If anything else was needed they would have most likely have provided that as well.

How did the women provide? The three women named as providers would have been women of means who possessed the resources to purchase goods. There were many other women who were disciples and they would have helped carry and manage the water supply, go to the market for supplies for meals, cook meals, obtain wool and leather for clothing and shoes, spin cloth and thread, hand sew clothing and shoes, and wash clothing when needed. Talk about having to be creative!

The disciples included the original twelve disciples, Jesus also sent out 72 disciples at one point, plus the women who traveled with Jesus. Some biblical historians believe by the end of Jesus' ministry there were 120 who traveled with him.

Jesus expelled seven demons from Mary Magdalene when he healed her. The seven demons would have represented 'numerous' demons and indicates there were many demons. Certainly Mary would have been tormented before she met Jesus and she would have had great relief and peace when Jesus healed and transformed her!

Creative provision would have been the norm for the women. If they needed something they had to figure out what they could use and how to make it. They didn't have patterns they could buy or cookbooks filled with recipes. They had to use create everything from raw materials.

The Greek word for provision or support is διακονέω pronounced diakoneo. The English root word stems from the Latin word providere meaning 'to foresee or attend to'.

The word breakdown is: pro meaning 'before' and videre meaning 'to see'. Mary and the female disciples supported Jesus as they creatively saw to their needs each day. As they traveled from town to town they did not have the resources to carry a lot of supplies or water (no SUV's available) so they depended on local markets for their needs.

Experience:

What is the most creative thing you've done from raw materials?

Food item, clothing? Shoes?

The women supplied all of those things for Jesus and the disciples.

Where would they have found the materials for shoes?

UNIT V

CHAPTER 13

YOUR GENIUS!

WOMAN OF VALOR MARY MAGDALENE

Matthew 27:27-56, Mark 15:21-38, Luke 23:26-49, and John 19:16-37 Matthew 27:55-56 (NLT)
And many women who had come from Galilee with Jesus to care for him were watching from a distance. Among them were Mary Magdalene, Mary (the mother of James and Joseph), and the mother of James and John, the sons of Zebedee.

Matthew 28:1-10 NLT
Early on Sunday morning, as the new day was dawning, Mary Magdalene and the other Mary went out to visit the tomb. Suddenly there was a great earthquake! For an angel of the Lord came down from heaven, rolled aside the stone, and sat on it. His face shone like lightning, and his clothing was as white as snow. The guards shook with fear when they saw him, and they fell into a dead faint. Then the angel spoke to the women. "Don't be afraid!" he said. "I know you are looking for Jesus, who was crucified. He isn't here! He is risen from the dead, just as he said would happen. Come, see where his body was lying. And now, go quickly and tell his disciples that he has risen from the dead, and he is going ahead of you to Galilee. You will see him there. Remember what I have told you." The women ran quickly from the tomb. They were very frightened but also filled with great joy, and they rushed to give the disciples the angel's message. And as they went, Jesus met them and greeted them. And they ran to him, grasped his feet, and worshiped him. Then Jesus said to them, "Don't be afraid! Go tell my brothers to leave for Galilee, and they will see me there."

Mark 15:40-41 and 47 (NLT)
Some women were there, watching from a distance, including Mary Magdalene, Mary (the mother of James the younger and of Joseph), and Salome. They had been followers of Jesus and had cared for him while he was in Galilee. Many other women who had come with him to Jerusalem were also there. Mary Magdalene and Mary the mother of Joseph saw where Jesus' body was laid.

Mark 16:1-7 (NLT)
Saturday evening, when the Sabbath ended, Mary Magdalene, Mary the mother of James, and Salome went out and purchased burial spices so they could anoint Jesus' body. Very early on Sunday morning, just at sunrise, they went to the tomb. On the way they were asking each other, "Who will roll away the stone for us from the entrance to the tomb?" But as they arrived, they looked up and saw that the stone, which was very large, had already been rolled aside. When they entered the tomb, they saw a young man clothed in a white robe sitting on the right side. The women were shocked, but the angel said, "Don't be alarmed. You are looking for Jesus of Nazareth, who was crucified. He isn't here! He is risen from the dead! Look, this is where they laid his body. Now go and tell his disciples, including Peter, that Jesus is going ahead of you to Galilee. You will see him there, just as he told you before he died."

Luke 23:55, 56 NLT
As his body was taken away, the women from Galilee followed and saw the tomb where his body was placed. Then they went home and prepared spices and ointments to anoint his body. But by the time they were finished the Sabbath had begun, so they rested as required by the law.

Luke 24:1-10 NLT
But very early on Sunday morning the women went to the tomb, taking the spices they had prepared. They found that the stone had been rolled away from the entrance. So they went in, but they didn't find the body of the Lord Jesus. As they stood there puzzled, two men suddenly appeared to them, clothed in dazzling robes. The women were terrified and bowed with their faces to the ground. Then the men asked, "Why are you looking among the dead for someone who is alive? He isn't here! He is risen from the dead! Remember what he told you back in Galilee, that the Son of Man must be betrayed into the hands of sinful men and be crucified, and that he would rise again on the third day." Then they remembered that he had said this. So they rushed back from the tomb to tell his eleven disciples—and everyone else—what had happened. It was Mary Magdalene, Joanna, Mary the mother of James, and several other women who told the apostles what had happened.

John 19:25-30 NLT
Standing near the cross were Jesus' mother, and his mother's sister, Mary (the wife of Clopas), and Mary Magdalene. When Jesus saw his mother standing there beside the disciple he loved, he said to her, "Dear woman, here is your son." And he said to this disciple, "Here is your mother." And from then on this disciple took her into his home. Jesus knew that his mission was now finished, and to fulfill Scripture he said, "I am thirsty." A jar of sour wine was sitting there, so they soaked a sponge in it, put it on a hyssop branch, and held it up to his lips. When Jesus had tasted it, he said, "It is finished!" Then he bowed his head and released his spirit.

John 20:1, 2, 4-9 NLT
Early on Sunday morning, while it was still dark, Mary Magdalene came to the tomb and found that the stone had been rolled away from the entrance. She ran and found Simon Peter and the other disciple, the one whom Jesus loved. She said, "They have taken the Lord's body out of the tomb, and we don't know where they have put him!" They were both running, but the other disciple outran Peter and reached the tomb first. He stooped and looked in and saw the linen wrappings lying there, but he didn't go in. Then Simon Peter arrived and went inside. He also noticed the linen wrappings lying there, while the cloth that had covered Jesus' head was folded up and lying apart from the other wrappings. Then the disciple who had reached the tomb first also went in, and he saw and believed— for until then they still hadn't understood the Scriptures that said Jesus must rise from the dead.

Mary Magdalene was still providing when Jesus was on the cross. She stayed at the cross with Jesus' mother until the body was taken down. According to the account in Luke 23:55-57 she went to buy spices for the body but by the time they were ready to anoint the body it was the Sabbath so she had to wait another day.

Mary's Genius was clearly in servant leadership. She had resources that she used for Jesus and his followers and she was liberal with her time. Whenever Jesus was in Galilee she was there serving Jesus and his disciples. Since feeding a crowd that size (between 70-120 people) would have been an all day affair (they fed them for every meal) we know she worked from dawn to dusk. She also would have taken time to listen to Jesus.

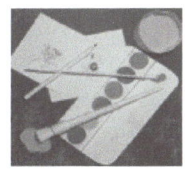

Albert Einstein believed, "Everybody is a genius. But if you judge a fish by its ability to climb a tree, it will live its whole life believing that it's stupid."

Exercise: What's your genius?

Combine passions, dreams, gifts, and experiences to determine if you are a fish trying to climb a tree or if you are a fish swimming in the ocean.

_____

_____

_____

_____

_____

UNIT VI CHAPTERS 14 AND 15
EXPLORING LEARNING

WOMAN OF VALOR
THE ADULTEROUS WOMAN

Proverbs 31:20

She extends a helping hand to the poor and opens her arms to the needy.

UNIT VI

CHAPTER 14

LEARNING
EXPLORATION
HOW WE THINK

WOMAN OF VALOR
THE ADULTEROUS WOMAN

Proverbs 31:20 (NLT)
She extends a helping hand to the poor and opens her arms to the needy.

John 8:2-6a (NLT)
Early the next morning he was back again at the Temple. A crowd soon gathered, and he sat down and taught them. As he was speaking, the teachers of religious law and the Pharisees brought a woman who had been caught in the act of adultery. They put her in front of the crowd. "Teacher," they said to Jesus, "this woman was caught in the act of adultery. The law of Moses says to stone her. What do you say?" They were trying to trap him into saying something they could use against him.

The Proverbs 31 woman is compassionate and loving wanting to help everyone, even those outside her inner circle. The poetic imagery used of 'helping hands' and 'open arms' is very powerful and inviting. This nurturing imagery helps us to understand we can fall into God's open arms and trust his strong hands to gently guide us. Throughout scripture God makes clear his heart for the poor and weary. God's heart is waiting for us to come!

When the Pharisees brought in the woman caught in adultery they were certain they could trick Jesus. Based on his past record of showing compassion on the downtrodden, they knew he would offer the same compassion to this woman. The problem is that the law, Torah, stipulated that adultery was a capital crime (Lev. 20:10) but the Roman Government outlawed Jewish rights to capital punishment in 30 AD. If Jesus upheld the Torah he could be charged by the Romans for breaking their law. If he didn't uphold the Torah the Pharisees would accuse him of breaking Jewish law. Either way Jesus was doomed, so reasoned the Pharisees.

Jesus knew the Pharisees were trying to trick him but that was undoubtedly not his greatest concern. His greatest concern was for the woman's restoration. Despite the fact that she had committed adultery, Jesus loved her and had compassion for her. Jesus was actually glad the Pharisees brought the woman to him. They could have simply taken her to the city gates and stoned her. There, everyone would have been willing to cast a stone at her.

You have a friend at church who is miserable with her marriage. She tells you she wants out, hoping you will understand knowing how unhappy she is in her marriage. You know she is unhappy, but you also know giving up easily is not God's choice for your friend. Condemning her will alienate her, but by accepting her choice to give up because she's unhappy you will be going against everything you believe is right. You feel like you are caught in between and both choices are lose-lose.

Learning to make decisions based on win-win is often difficult to do because most of the time our feelings are involved. When we have deep feelings for someone, the thought of loss is difficult to deal with. Even professionals who are involved personally struggle when the person in question is a close friend or a family member. That's not to say it's impossible, just difficult.

Jesus was faced with a very difficult decision, and the Pharisees had him backed into a corner. In light of what they were trying to trap him into doing, Jesus knew he needed to get to the heart of the matter. That realization which he made clear to the Pharisees included the condition of their own hearts and minds. Jesus reminded them that YHWH is a God of mercy and forgiveness. That included their sins but he first needed Them to recognize they had sins as well.

Let me be clear here...Jesus wasn't trying to trap them in return. He wanted to restore them into relationship with God. The Pharisees were not Jesus' enemies. They were misguided Jews who needed God's love. They had taken the law and poisoned it with legalism and judgment. Jesus was just as concerned for their spiritual well-being as that of the woman. He loved them and wanted them to recognize they needed God because they weren't perfect either.

I was broken-hearted when I saw the woman the Pharisees threw on the ground that day. Their eyes were filled with self-righteous indignation. As I looked at her, this poor woman who had been treated all her life like garbage, I saw the woman she could be. I remembered her as a child laughing and gently helping her mother with the younger children. I saw the cruel man her parents pledged her to and felt her dashed hopes of ever being loved. I saw the gentle man who reached out to her, actually treating her like a human being. Yes, she should not have committed adultery, but she didn't do it to spite her husband. She just wanted to be loved. It broke my heart that the Pharisees didn't see her! They only saw the law, their expanded and twisted version of God's law. The problem with their version of the law is that they stripped God's love and mercy away leaving a set of rules and regulations. God never intended for the Law to be treated as a tool for power and indignation. God intended for the Law to serve as a reminder of his love and desire to guide his children. Now the woman lay at my feet, a stone's throw away from dying. I cared for her, but I also cared for the Pharisees and wanted them to see the Law as it was intended to be!

Experience:
Have you ever noticed the word RESTORATION?
REST in God
Receive God's STORehouse of love.
God's RATION of manna is available for you today.
Take time to receive God's RESTORATION.

UNIT VI

CHAPTER 15

LEARNING EXPLORATION

CHANGING ATTITUDES

WOMAN OF VALOR
THE ADULTEROUS WOMAN

Proverbs 31:20
She extends a helping hand to the poor and opens her arms to the needy.

John 8:6b-11
Jesus stooped down and wrote in the dust with his finger. They kept demanding an answer, so he stood up again and said, "All right, but let the one who has never sinned throw the first stone!" Then he stooped down again and wrote in the dust. When the accusers heard this, they slipped away one by one, beginning with the oldest, until only Jesus was left in the middle of the crowd with the woman. Then Jesus stood up again and said to the woman, "Where are your accusers? Didn't even one of them condemn you?" "No, Lord," she said. And Jesus said, "Neither do I. Go and sin no more." (NLT)

What was Jesus writing in the dirt? Theologians have speculated for centuries about Jesus' message in the dirt. I find that the absolute best message we can give each other is, "Jesus loves me, this I know for the Bible tells me so." Jesus wanted the woman to ask for and receive forgiveness. He wanted the Pharisees to receive God's love. He wanted them to love each other. "Jesus loves me" speaks eons to people lost in a dying world. There is no better gift we can offer than, Jesus loves YOU.

Don't you just hate it when someone is badgering you for an answer? I think it's highly possible that Jesus was trying to give them time to 'get a clue'. He was hoping they would stop long enough to think it through and realize their scheme to trap him was a trap they had set for themselves. They were sowing judgment and pain and that's exactly what they would reap. Jesus knew whatever was in their hearts would come back to them. Anytime we judge others, we are really judging ourselves. When we don't offer mercy, we don't give ourselves mercy. When we refuse to forgive, we do not forgive ourselves. That isn't what Jesus wanted for the woman or the Pharisees. He wanted them to sow forgiveness and mercy so they would receive forgiveness and mercy.

Jesus made it clear that we need to "notice the log" in our own eye (Matthew 7:3). It really does require a change of attitude...complete change. Instead of focusing on the other person's faults we turn the focus to how we can best love that person. Oftentimes we are trying to make someone else look bad so we will look good (or at least better). That would indicate we have a spiritual problem within ourselves, about ourselves. When that is the case we need to ask God to help us love ourselves and accept our faults. Since God forgives us, we need to get a clue and forgive ourselves and others.

Oh how Jesus prayed for them as he wrote in the dirt that day. He prayed they would see the woman's heart. He prayed that the Pharisees would receive all God had for them. Jesus wanted them to change their attitudes so they would be loving and gracious. God never intends that decisions we make are made out of strife or judgment. God's intention is that we love, really love one another and forgive. Jesus' prayer for you is that you will love one another, forgive, and rely on God for restoration. Really, it's the greatest gift you can give yourself.

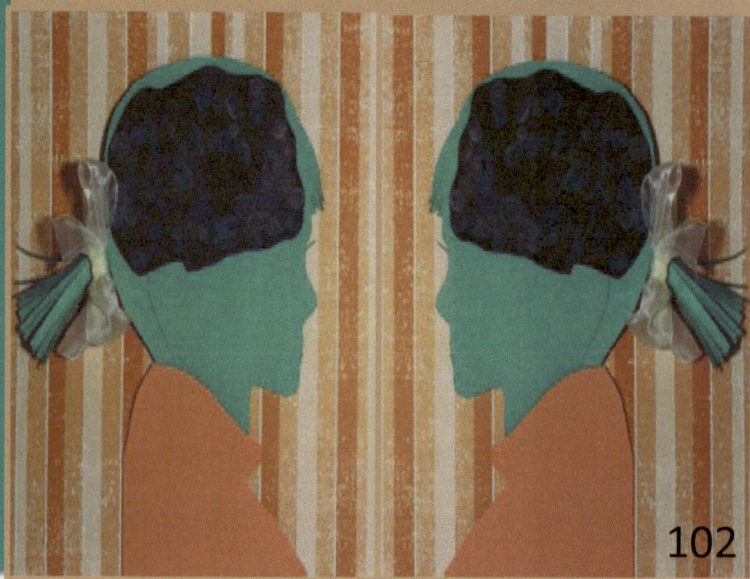

Slip Sliding Away…one by one the Pharisees walked away. They were probably trying to look for a hole in Jesus' statement, but finding none they eventually disappeared from sight. What they had sown in hatred and ugliness was now a heap of hatred and ugliness within themselves. Still, Jesus didn't want that for them. He wanted, still wanted to give them love and life. He desperately wanted them to believe in his love and forgiveness.

Experience: Forgiveness is a daily endeavor. Sometimes the pain is very deep and peeling back the layers takes time. God gives us time. God is gracious and loving and as each layer comes off we forgive for the pain we've uncovered. Because God doesn't expect us to experience all of the pain at one time, he gently uncovers some of the pain so we can forgive and receive God's restoration. Spend time with God today, forgive (even if you don't feel like it) and give your pain to God. Give God time to restore you.

UNIT VII LOVE AND FAITH

ANNA

WOMAN OF VALOR

Proverbs 31:10

Who can find a virtuous and capable wife? She is more precious than rubies.

UNIT VII

CHAPTER 16

LOVE

WOMAN OF VALOR ANNA

Luke 2:36-37
Anna, a prophet, was also there in the Temple. She was the daughter of Phanuel from the tribe of Asher, and she was very old. Her husband died when they had been married only seven years. Then she lived as a widow to the age of eighty-four. She never left the Temple but stayed there day and night, worshiping God with fasting and prayer.

Proverbs 31:10 to 31

It's clear that love is laced throughout Proverbs 31:10-31. God's wise nurturing love is ever present in our lives and shows up sometimes when we least expect it. The poem speaks of the many things daily that are done in love for husband, children, maidens, and all who enter the city gates.

The Lord does indeed bless through his gracious love and daily care.

God's greatest desire is that we will receive all he has in store for us!

Woman of Valor
Anna

Anna was a blessing and a surprise to Mary and Joseph.

When they went to the Temple that day they would not have expected to be greeted by a loving gracious woman who was waiting for their arrival!

She had waited for this child to come. While she waited, she loved well and spent time praying and talking to God about the Messiah.

It's no wonder that the instant she laid eyes on the child she knew he was the one God sent to save the world!

She knew because she spent a lifetime in intimate fellowship with the Father.

She knew because God's love permeated her heart and soul. She knew because the Spirit was alive and well IN Anna, this Prophetess.

How long had Anna waited? We know she was 84 years old and that she was married for only 7 years.

At that time, it was not unusual for a girl at 13 to marry, and much of the time she would have been pledged to an older man. Men were allowed to marry when they could prove they could provide for a wife. That meant in some cases the men were much older than the women. If Anna married at 13 and her husband died when she was 20 years old that means she had lived in the Temple praying and waiting for the Messiah for 64 years!

Certainly her waiting was not in vain and her prayers were woven in *love*.

Anna possessed great love, strength of character, and is a powerful symbol of God's love. God IN us is chayill. As human women we ourselves do not possess chayill, but with God in us we possess unlimited resources of chayill. Because God is IN us (God is not just somewhere out there in heaven but he resides IN us) all of the resources God has are ours. They are already here IN us. We simply need to recognize what God is blessing in us and receive God's chayill.

Anna was an excellent, virtuous woman of strength.

The Hebrew word for virtuous/excellent is:
חַיִל
pronounced chayill Chayill can mean great strength, great wealth, valient, powerful, or efficient. The key here is that the poem is describing a woman who is fiercely blessed with capable qualities and gifts.

The pronunciation of the work emits a powerful sound that speaks volumes of strength. The beginning consonant begins in the very back part of the throat - just like it sounds when you are clearing your throat then you spit out a hard H followed by a soft ai sound. The final sounds - yil - trail off to end but the Y is clearly enunciated. The point is, it's even a powerful sounding word!

What is most amazing about Anna is that scripture says she did not ever leave the Temple. She had been IN the Temple day and night for decades! She did not go to market. She did not go to visit friends. She did not go to the city gate. She stayed in the Temple.

FASTING

She spent all of her time fasting and praying for the Messiah! To point out that she fasted and prayed would have meant she gave up food to show her dependence o God and her submission to God's will. From the time of the Exile to the time of Jesus fasting was thought of as a pious act and a powerful way to pray. Certainly, fasting is practiced today as a sign of submission and is recognized as a powerful means of praying. While fasting, you do tend to become weaker in body and spirit and more dependent on God.

Anna spent her life praying and fasting she possibly would have only eaten enough to sustain her life.

If you FAST

Common practice is to drink a lot of water while fasting.

If fasting a lot, it is not suggested that you eat rich foods but that you rely on a simple diet when the fast is over.

Ancient Israel

Women in Ancient Israel lived in a patriarchal world but they were given status equal to men in the eyes of God. Eve was given to Adam as his helper and mutual companion. There were female prophetess' in the Old Testament but only a few were prominent enough to be named (Exodus 15:20, 2 Kings 22:14-20, Judges 4-5, Nehemiah 6:14, Ezekiel 13:7, and Joel 2:28.)

Women were not excluded from worshiping God, were honored as being models of wisdom, nurturers, had protected rights (Genesis 16:5-6, 38) and if gifted would be allowed to engage in a business of her own in ancient Israel.

Old Testament scripture shows God is fiercely protective of women who are widowed or not married and of women who do not have children to care for them in their old age. Likewise, God protects the poor and broken (both men and women) and orphaned children. Young women were considered to be under the protection of their fathers until married. Parents played an active role in choosing a spouse for their daughters. It helps us to understand how great a role they played when we realize girls often married very young. Certainly, a young girl would rely on her parents to make a wise choice that would take her well-being into account.

After the Babylonian Exile

Women's roles changed somewhat after the exile from Egypt but especially during and after the Babylonian Exile (mostly took place around 597 BCE) when the priests put plans in place to ensure Israel would follow the law while exiled. Women were already excluded from circumcision and came under the protection of fathers/husbands. When the priests put purity rules in place, women were excluded from society during menstruation and childbirth. During that time they were considered to be unclean. Women became more excluded from worship and only had access to the Temple through their husbands.

At the time Anna was born there would have been an outer court for women which was outside of the sanctuary. Any vow a woman made could be reversed by her husband, women were excluded from testifying in court, and they were not to be educated. Anna's choice to live in the Temple after she lost her husband would have most likely been approved by the man who had charge over her. If her husband had brothers they could take on that role, or she could possibly have gone back to her father's house (remember Ruth who was urged by Naomi to return to her father's house). At any rate, the decision was made to honor her choice and she was allowed to live a life dedicated to prayer.

Experience:

Set aside time to fast and pray. If you have never fasted, do so carefully (don't start by doing a water only fast). Jeremiah did vegetable fasts and only ate vegetables and water. There are many other kinds of fasts.

It is also advisable to start out slowly (unless the Spirit tells you differently) and to do a dawn to dusk fast or a 1 day 24 hour fast.
The point of fasting is to spend extra time praying so make sure you set aside time to spend listening to God.

As you conclude your fasting and prayer time do not eat a large meal. Your first meal should be small and simple (no rich foods). Your digestive system needs to be gently acclimated back to eating regular foods.

WOMAN OF VALOR

CHAPTER 17

GOD'S FAITHFULESS

WOMAN OF VALOR
ANNA

Proverbs 31:10b

...She is more precious than rubies

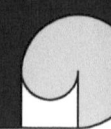

Anna had lived in the Temple for decades and spent all of her time fasting and praying for the coming Messiah. Simeon, a Prophet also lived in Jerusalem at the time of Jesus' birth and the Holy Spirit had revealed to Simeon that he would not die until he saw the Messiah. The Spirit led Simeon to the Temple the day Joseph and Mary went to present Jesus to fulfill what was required by Jewish Law. Simeon immediately knew Jesus was the Messiah. As Anna came upon Simeon talking to Mary ad Joseph she also immediately knew that this was the Christ child. Can you imagine how Anna felt after praying and fasting for around 60 years when her prayers were answered? Her heart was bursting with joy and she began worshiping and praising God for sending the Messiah!

Anna would have been considered to be pious and faithful because she chose to remain a widow. When you add to that the fact that she spent her life in the Temple and she spent all of her time fasting and praying, she would have been known as 'Anna the Faithful'. Because she was widowed while young and no children are mentioned, her life was solely dedicated to praying for the coming Messiah. She believed the Messiah would come.

Luke 2:38-40
She came along just as Simeon was talking with Mary and Joseph, and she began praising God. She talked about the child to everyone who had been waiting expectantly for God to rescue Jerusalem. When Jesus' parents had fulfilled all the requirements of the law of the Lord, they returned home to Nazareth in Galilee. There the child grew up healthy and strong. He was filled with wisdom, and God's favor was on him.
(NLT)

WHENEVER WE LOOK AT FAITH IT IS IMPORTANT TO DEFINE IT IN TERMS OF SCRIPTURE AND NOT IN TERMS OF THE MODERN (20TH CENTURY) VIEW OF FAITH.

In Genesis 15:6 the word for faith is: אָמַן pronounced aman. The verb means to support, confirm, or be faithful.

In Genesis 15 God promises Abram he will have children and in response to the promise Abram believes God. The response is confirmation of God's word. In other words, Abram did not decide himself that he would have children. He did not choose that promise. It was God who promised God who chose, and God who gave his word to Abram allowing him to believe.

Hebrews 11:1 Faith is the confidence that what we hope for will actually happen; it gives us assurance about things we cannot see.

LOVE ~~HATRED~~

JOY ~~SADNESS~~

HOPE ~~DESPAIR~~

FAITH ~~DOUBT~~

"So faith comes from hearing, that is, hearing the Good News about Christ. (NLT).

Anna's faith came from hearing God the Spirit speak to her about the Christ. God moved her heart and she received the message of the coming Christ child.

If you had waited for 60+ years to see the Messiah, would you keep his coming silent? Probably not. Anna was so overcome by the presence of the child that she told everyone she had seen the Messiah. The one she had prayed for and waited for had come and she was not at all silent about it.

She also imparted the message to everyone she came in contact with that this child was going to 'rescue' Jerusalem (her world as she knew it). Rescue from what? What were they in need of being rescued from? Most likely many she spoke with believed they would be rescued from the cruel Roman government, from high taxes, and from lack of resources. Life at the time of Jesus was difficult.

King Herod was busy building a kingdom that would make him look great to the Roman Empire and as a result, taxes were levied so he could build grand structures and offer bribes when needed (which was often). The people Anna spoke with would not have found hope in a spiritual kingdom.

They wanted hope NOW. The disciples were no different. They believed Jesus would establish an earthly kingdom that would them from Roman rule. Anna however thought of none of that. She believed in the word God gave her and that word would have been more encompassing than helping them survive the Roman Empire. The message that Anna shouted out was a message of hope and freedom. She believed God's faithful promise that ONE would come as Savior.

Anna was faithful to wait and faithful to proclaim the Messiah had come.

The Apostle Paul tells of the fruit of the Spirit in Galatians 5:22, and one of the fruit (evidences) is faithfulness. Having faithfulness is evidence of the fact that we have heard and receive the gift of believing. Just as Simeon heard the promise that he would see the Messiah in his lifetime, just as Anna prayed and fasted that the Messiah would come, we are encouraged to listen (hear) the message and receive God's promises.

WHETHER YOU ARE SISTER, MOTHER, AUNT, NEIGHBOR, WIFE, OR CO-WORKER, YOU ARE A PRECIOUS PRICELESS GIFT FROM GOD. YOU ARE TO BE CHERISHED!

THE PROVERBS 31 WOMAN HAD CHARACTER THAT WAS SAID TO BE OF GREATER VALUE THAN RUBIES OR PEARLS. THOSE WERE PRECIOUS STONES THAT WERE ONLY AVAILABLE TO KINGS OR THE VERY WEALTHY AT THE TIME PROVERBS WAS WRITTEN.

Anna told everyone that she had seen the Christ, it was her natural response to tell of God's love and grace. Telling should not be forced or awkward but should be a natural response to the world. Telling is Spirit led and listening is an important component of telling. Just as Anna prayed and fasted, we too should pray and even fast for those in our circle who do not know about God's love and grace.

COMMON PEOPLE DID NOT OWN PRECIOUS STONES SO TO SAY TO A MAN THAT HIS WIFE IS MORE PRECIOUS THAN RUBIES MEANT SHE IS PRICELESS. THE AUTHOR WAS TELLING HIS READERS THAT THIS IS A GIFT THEY MIGHT NEVER BE ABLE TO AFFORD. SHE, WOMAN IS THE GIFT. SHE, WOMAN IS THE PRICELESS STONE. SHE IS WISE, HAS CHARACTER, IS FAITHFUL AND LOVING, AND IS THE MOST PRECIOUS GIFT GOD GIVES TO MAN.

Experience: The Proverbs 31 woman represents God-like qualities that are part of our DNA. No woman possesses all of those qualities, but women together possess those qualities. Name your quality and list qualities of female friends, co-workers, family members who possess those qualities. Together women are strong and learning to rely on each other's strengths and gifts is part of what makes the church, CHURCH.

Proverbs 31:10-31
Matthew, Mark, Luke, and John

General Prayer of Charity by Charles Dickens:

Make us O Lord remember that
it is Christianity to do good always,
even to those who do evil to us,
to love our neighbor as ourselves,
and to do to all men as we would
have them do to us; to be gentle,
merciful and forgiving, and to keep
those qualities quiet in our own
hearts and never make a boast of
them; but always to show that we
love Thee by humbly trying to do
the right in everything; that thus
remembering the life and lessons
of our Lord Jesus Christ and try to
act up to them, we may confidently
hope that Thou wilt forgive us our
sins and mistakes and enable us
to live to die in peace through
Jesus Christ our Lord. Amen

Woman of Valor: A Restorative Journey

The Blessing of Thankfulness

The Psalms of David are an ever present reminder of understanding being thankful in the midst of all of the circumstances of life. Even in our darkest hour, we have the promise that God is always present, always faithful, and always acting on our behalf through His gracious love.

The Apostle Paul wrote to the church in Rome (Romans 5:1-5) telling them, "Therefore, since we have been made right in God's sight by faith, we have peace with God because of what Jesus Christ our Lord has done for us. Because of our faith, Christ has brought us into this place of undeserved privilege where we now stand, and we confidently and joyfully look forward to sharing God's glory.

We can rejoice, too, when we run into problems and trials, for we know that they help us develop endurance, and endurance develops strength of character, and character strengthens our confident hope of salvation. And this hope will not lead to disappointment. For we know how dearly God loves us, because He has given us the Holy Spirit to fill our hearts with His love." (NLT)

Every woman we've "met" in our journey through Woman of Valor encountered pain and sorrow and in the midst of their trials they were restored through Jesus' love and gracious forgiveness.

Who are we called to be as women? Thankful servants, restored by grace and covered by God's faithful love. You, my sister are God's special gem, a pearl of great price bought an paid for by His only Son. You are worth more than gold!

O Lord, we are restored by Your love, Your forgiveness, and the touch of Your mighty hand.

www.ingramcontent.com/pod-product-compliance
Lightning Source LLC
Chambersburg PA
CBHW042028150426
43198CB00003B/97